James Campbell was born in ~~...~~ 1982 he was editor of the *New Edinburgh* ~~...~~ works for the *Times Literary Supplement*. He is the author of *Invisible Country: A journey through Scotland* (1984).

In order to write *Gate Fever* James Campbell spent four months talking to the inmates of Lewes prison – a high-security prison containing fifty life-sentence prisoners, fifty long-termers and another fifty short-termers. Only after much difficulty was he granted access to the prison and permission to write a book about it. The result brings together an unusual chorus of voices: murderers, fraudsters, armed robbers, some wrongly imprisoned men, as well as the 'trusties', 'nonces', 'grassers' and even the 'screws'. *Gate Fever* is a vivid and accurate description of life behind bars.

'He has saved them from silence' SUNDAY TELEGRAPH

GATE FEVER

Voices from a prison

JAMES CAMPBELL

SPHERE BOOKS LIMITED

Sphere Books Limited, 27 Wrights Lane, London W8 5TZ

First published in Great Britain by Weidenfeld & Nicolson Ltd 1986
Copyright © 1986 James Campbell
First published by Sphere Books Ltd 1987

TRADE
MARK

Set in 9/11 Linotron Sabon

Printed and bound in Great Britain by
Collins, Glasgow

For Fanny Dubes

Their whispered dialogue grazes the silence of this hell without breaking it — a low-flying bird seems thus to graze the water — searching into *the meaning of life*. . . . And perhaps in that instant they are the only men in this jail, in this city, in this part of the universe, in whom the inexplicable flame of pure thought flickers.

VICTOR SERGE,
Men in Prison

Caliban (to Prospero): You taught me language; and my profit on't is, I know how to curse.

The Tempest

Contents

THE NEW PRISON LEWES: FOR THE EASTERN DIVISION OF THE COUNTY OF SUSSEX

1 CELLS.

2 OFFICERS.

3 TRADE INSTRUCTORS ROOM.

4 SURGERY.

5 CORRIDOR.

6 INSPECTION HALL.

7 PRISONERS VISITING ROOMS.

8 MAGISTRATES ROOM.

9 SURGEONS BED ROOM.

10 SURGEONS PARLOUR.

11 WAITING ROOM.

12 GOVERNORS OFFICE.

13 GOVERNORS CLERKS OFFICE.

14 SOLICITORS ROOM.

15 CHIEF WARDERS BED ROOM.

16 CHIEF WARDERS SITTING ROOM.

17 INFIRMARY WARD.

18 INFIRMARY WARDER.

19 DEBTORS DAY ROOM.

20 MATRONS BED ROOM.

21 MATRONS PARLOUR.

22 ENTRANCE.

23 DAY ROOM 1ST CLASS DEBTORS.

24 DAY ROOM 2ND CLASS DEBTORS.

25 INCLINED PLANE.

26 INFIRMARY AIRING YARD.

27 DRYING YARD.

28 INFIRMARY AIRING YARD.

29 DEBTORS AIRING YARD.

30 ENTRANCE COURT.

31 AIRING YARD 1ST CLASS DEBTORS.

32 AIRING YARD 2ND CLASS DEBTORS.

33 AIRING YARD 3RD CLASS DEBTORS.

34 GATEWAY.

35 PORTERS LODGE.

The original ground-plan of Lewes Prison

Prisoners from the old House of Correction were transferred, according to the minutes of the Building Committee, on 15 August 1853. Subsidiary buildings and extensions of the wall have increased its overall size, but the prison as it is today remains fundamentally true to this plan. The detached wing which was used to contain females now holds remand prisoners, while the one reserved for 'Debtors' is today the prison hospital. C Wing is the eastward horizontal spar of the cross; the author's cell was at the top right-hand corner of the short wing marked 'Vagrants'.

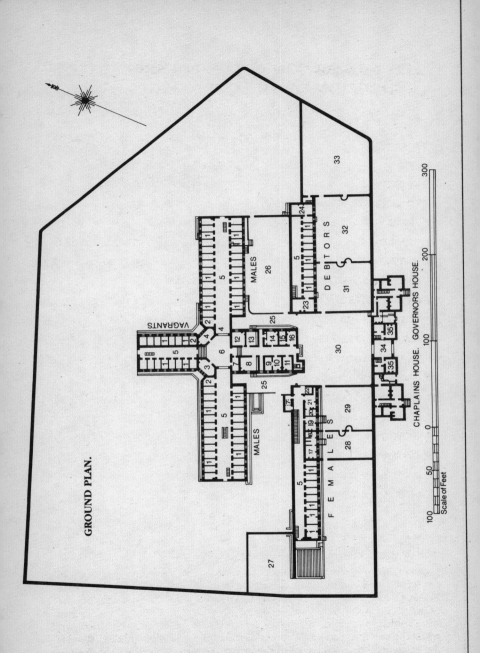

GROUND PLAN.

Preface

This is a book about men in prison. It is based on a year's acquaintance with the prisoners and staff of Lewes Prison's C Wing: in particular on the four months, between November 1984 and March 1985, during which I went into the prison daily.

Lewes Prison has a threefold function: to contain convicted prisoners – many of them of the second-highest security rank, Category B – in a closed training prison; to serve as a local prison for men serving short sentences; and to hold remand prisoners, both over and under twenty-one, until they are brought to trial. I chose to overlook the last of these functions and devote my attention to the convicts – the 'serving men'. C Wing contains a mixture of long-term, short-term and life-sentence prisoners. Lewes was chosen as a setting for no reason other than that its Governor was the first to welcome my approach and to offer, unconditionally, the facilities and freedom of movement I required.

What follows has no aspiration to be regarded as sociology or criminology, but as a writer's report on the life of a single prison constructed from notes, tape-recordings and memory. It emerges from encounters mainly with prisoners, and also with prison officers and others whose daily business takes them inside the prison. In many instances prisoners allude to their crimes and to the circumstances of their confinement, but these references were seldom prompted; almost all our conversations began in a casual manner and developed according to mood. While I never forgot that I was dealing with him the law had deemed a criminal, I always recognized him as a man first and an outlaw second.

All prisoners' names, except one, and those of most officers, have been changed.

I would like to acknowledge here the assistance of Denis Brown, who left his post as Governor of Lewes Prison in July 1985 for another elsewhere in the Prison Department; the forbearance of Ian Porter of the same department; the hospitality of Sheila Rennie; and the invaluable encouragement of Hilary Davies.

1. Prison Town

HM Prison Lewes is perched on a rise at the south-western tip of the East Sussex county town, beyond the original boundaries, on the road to Brighton. It was built according to a design which, since the Pentonville experiment of 1842 to replace the Hulks and houses of correction with 'model prisons', had become the standard one for prison architecture in the nineteenth century: several wings radiating from a central hub, forming either a star or a cross. Lewes, with four wings comprising the main body, is designed in the image of the cross, which, to the ecclesiastically minded superiors in charge at the time, might have had satisfying suggestions of redemption through punishment. Now, in keeping with the shrunken faith in the reforming function of a prison sentence, the symbolism, if any, stops at punishment.

Daniel Defoe called Lewes 'a fine pleasant town, well built and well situated', and the simple description holds good today. Eight miles from the south coast, built in a hollow of the South Downs through which the River Ouse runs to meet the sea at Newhaven, with a population of 15,000, it is one of the prettiest towns of its size in England. It boasts an impressive list of notable residents, from Thomas Paine, who never saw the inside of any of its prisons, to Mick Jagger, who did.

The approach to the prison, up the steeply sloping High Street, is comparitively unaltered since the eighteenth century. Most of the houses are Georgian, well preserved and brightly painted in an assortment of colours, and there are several older, timber-framed buildings which add quaintness to elegance. The town is dominated by a Norman castle, begun in 1100 and built on two artificial mounds, of which there remain a flint keep, a fourteenth-century barbican, or gatehouse, and a medieval tilting ground which has been converted into a bowling green.

At first sight the face of the prison, which stands a quarter of a mile further on up the hill at a slightly higher level than the castle, is not an especially ugly outsider in this company. Tourists are rumoured to have strolled up to its wooden gate and asked the price of admission, having mistaken it for the castle.

It was designed in 1852 by D.R. Hill, an architect imported from

Birmingham to do the job, and building began in the same year. The front is flinted with red-brick dressings, and twin, flat-topped towers flank the main gate. Adjoining the towers on each side are the two blocks which originally held the residences of the governor and the chaplain. These have now been converted into, on the right, a suite of offices for the governor and, where the governor's house once was, the officers' mess, with canteen, television lounge and snooker hall. On the far side of the governor's offices is the car park for employees, and next to the mess, a simple wooden tea-room has been constructed for the use of prisoners' visitors, some of whom arrive too early to be admitted or, on the way out, may have an hour to spare before catching the train back to London and beyond.

Between the prison facade and the Brighton road, which passes it, is a sloping lawn with a barricade of yew, pine and birch trees; from the cells on the top landings on the road-facing side it is possible to see over them to a clear view of the Sussex Downs.

The inner buildings are surrounded by a heptagonal high wall, and the large amounts of yard space created thereby are used to house subsidiary buildings and extensions to the main cross, such as the reception block, the education unit, the kitchen, the hospital, the church and several work-shops, and also for exercise yards, basketball and football pitches and the small prison aviary.

In the building of the prison 5,300 tons of flint were used, and the total cost was £56,097. (Of that, £164 was needed to prepare the road in front, whereas the cost of providing locks was £350.) It was designed to hold about three hundred prisoners; now, with doubling up in the two remand wings, the population is closer to five hundred.

Compared to the larger prisons of, for example, London – Wandsworth, Wormwood Scrubs, Brixton, with their electronic doors and intense, all-round security – Lewes has a relaxed atmosphere, although it is a Category B prison, which is in part a reflection of its parent town. The perimeter security, though it is high, is more subtle than at these other places: rolls of razor-blade wire frill the heights all round, including some potentially advantageous ones inside, but on the town side a curtain wall shields the wire-topped wall of the prison proper; there are no dogs, and no sterile or 'no-go' areas close to the inside wall, as there are at other prisons. Surveillance cameras have only lately been installed, and although their purpose is as much to intimidate as to guard, they do so discreetly.

The prison has undergone several changes of category since convicts from the old House of Correction in North Street were transferred to 'The

New Prison Lewes: For the Eastern Division of the County of Sussex', on 15 August 1853. A variety of types came from the old jail: debtors, female prisoners, vagrants, 'misdemeanants of the first class' and prisoners awaiting execution.

Such was the character of its population until the end of the century, after which it was used for a brief period as a borstal, then as a local prison; between 1917 and 1931 it was closed down. Now it contains, in effect, three prisons in one: a wing for adult remand prisoners awaiting trial (F Wing); another for young offenders – known as YPs, or young prisoners – under twenty-one (A Wing); and C Wing, a high-security training wing, housing 140 prisoners, divided into three classes: roughly fifty men doing life sentences, another fifty long-termers – serving upwards of four years – and the remainder, short-termers, doing less. It was to this wing that I restricted my interest.[1]

It took six months of sporadic negotiation before I succeeded in gaining the position I sought inside a closed training prison, first with the Press Office of the Prison Department at the Home Office, then with the Governor and the Prison Officers' Association at Lewes Prison, and then again with the Prison Department in pursuit of the higher authority's approval after Lewes had opened its doors to me.

After showing a polite but restrained interest in my approach, the Prison Department proved unable, or unwilling, to provide what it called 'accommodation' within a prison. At first it foresaw practical difficulties. My intention was to mix freely with prisoners, so far as the system allowed, and with a view to being accepted as a familiar fixture. The Prison Department's plans for me would have ruled out that possibility. According to its Press Officer, it would be necessary to have a member of staff assigned to escort me 'at all times'. Not only would this make my own movements cumbersome, it would also, obviously, affect the tenor of every conversation I had with a prisoner. From the point of view of the Prison Department, all this would be a further burden on a workforce which presents itself as heavily overburdened already.

As discussions continued, even this stinted method of accommodating me inside a prison began to seem too difficult; the physical danger I would be in was outlined, and it became clear to me that attempts to progress this way would be futile. That gate had closed.

I was left with the choice of dropping the idea, of approaching the

[1] After my term was completed the space for holding YPs was reduced and that for containing short-term prisoners expanded.

entrance by another route, or of putting my request to the Director of Prisons in Scotland, which has a separate administration. A Scottish prison would have been my first preference anyway, since I am Scottish myself. But when I suggested the project, it was rejected outright. Finally, when I was losing hope, Stephen Shaw of the Prison Reform Trust suggested contacting prison governors directly. Of course, nothing could be done without Home Office approval, but with a willing governor this blessing might be more easily attained.

Denis Brown, the Governor of Lewes Prison, was one of the first I contacted. He referred my request to visit the prison to the Home Office, which granted it, and then invited me down – in a phrase which sounded reassuring after the difficulties of the past months – 'to spend the afternoon and evening with us'.

Denis Brown welcomed me inside the main gate in the prison yard, hands clasped in front of him, a cross between a Sunday School teacher and a friendly policeman. He was formally polite, deliberate of speech, barely wasting a sentence, but was also possessed of an impish humour – an aspect of a strong will which often ran mildly counter to official policy.

He led the way into his office. It was large, with three long, arched, barred windows overlooking the Sussex Downs. When the sun flooded through it left three elongated, barred shadows across the floor before his desk.

It is the governor's task to receive policy from the Home Office and interpret it according to his own experience and imagination. Denis Brown said that when he arrived to take charge of Lewes – his first posting at the head of an establishment after many years of being involved in the running of young offenders' institutions at a slightly lower level – he found a 'self-confident' group of prison officers, but a prison which was somewhat stagnant and remote from the local community, and he resolved to encourage 'flexibility and growth'.

After we had talked for only a short time he surprised me by offering to provide the facilities I was looking for inside Lewes Prison. I told him I would require a room of my own where any prisoner could come and talk on any subject at any time (outside lock-up periods) without supervision; permission to tape certain conversations, with the prisoner's consent; and permission to come into the prison at any time on a daily basis for an indefinite period. Mr Brown foresaw no difficulty in acceding to these conditions and, after several subsequent meetings at which small but delicate points were ironed out with the Prison Officers' Association and a representative of the Home Office – including an invitation, politely declined, to sign the Official Secrets Act – he issued me a pass which enabled me to move freely about the prison without escort. Fears for my safety and phrases such as 'excessive commitments on staff time' were never mentioned, and I made my first appearance in C Wing on a drab November morning.

I was given a room on B Wing, the short upper spar of the cross which for general purposes is discussed as if it were a part of C Wing – a cell, fourteen by seven, with a vaulted ceiling and a small window high up on the back wall. It was used once a week by the barber who allowed my table, two chairs and small filing cabinet to share the floor space with his high chair, broom and bag of clippings. The only substantial alteration from the time when it was occupied by a prisoner was the glass door, which, to prevent barricading, did not lock from the inside. The window, hardly large enough for a small child to slip through, was shielded by two sets of bars and a layer of wire netting, this last protection being required to keep out the pigeons which came every day and warbled on the ledge.

Over the next four months I installed myself in the cramped cell, always too hot or too cold, five days a week. Sometimes I was there from nine o'clock in the morning until the lock-up at 8.30 p.m. To the frame of my door I tacked a notice (are tacks allowed? – it's the sort of question you begin asking yourself) giving my name and my reasons for being in the prison, and inviting anyone, prisoner or prison officer, who felt like doing so to come and talk. It was my intention, at least at first, to let them come to me. Ostentatious advances on my part could be misconstrued and might place me under suspicion of a kind it was essential to avoid, but once a man had crossed the threshold of my room he would be obliged to talk, if only about the weather.

Before long, the daily journey to and from London became too strenuous and time-consuming, so I rented a house in a narrow street opposite the police station, where I stayed for most of the next four months. The house was comfortable and small: it had three storeys but only one tiny room on each. The living room was triangular, with about as much space as a large car. It belonged to a former student of Russian who spent most of her time in London. In the evenings, after returning tired out from being a listener in the prison, I sat and read Chekhov, Gogol and Dostoevsky's *Memoirs from the House of the Dead*, about his experience in a Siberian prison, listening to music on a badly received Radio 3, across which police messages crackled with merciless and startling intrusiveness.

On my first morning there were few signs of anything, except the unusual uniforms, to suggest that one was not in an army barracks, or a hospital, or a school for overgrown boys. I left the door of my cell open as I arranged the few pieces of furniture, trying not to seem as if rejecting the attention my presence was already attracting. No one had introduced me or even given notice of my arrival to the prisoners; I simply appeared.

On the road up to the prison from the railway station an hour before, I had suddenly thought of several good reasons why I should not be doing this, and wished myself, as one does when approaching the dentist's chair, into a future when it would all be over. I did not expect prison to be a welcoming environment, which, in many strange and unpredictable ways, it turned out to be.

At 11.20 a.m. the dinner trolleys clattered past my door on their way from the kitchen to the hot-plate in B Wing where the meals were served. A slight man with blue eyes set in a shrivelled face topped by a crew cut detached himself from the queue and helped me with the office furniture – the first of many acts of kindness.

He was from New Zealand, he said. I said I was from Glasgow. Oh, Glasgow? He did his first bit of bird in Glasgow, he said. We had something in common, then. He told me a tale of deserting from the Foreign Legion, stowing away in a ship and turning up in the Glasgow docks a week later in his pyjamas, and having his story and picture printed in a Glasgow newspaper. (I tracked it down later, thirty-three years old, in a defunct evening paper: 'Here he is – George Robert Watson, whose life has given him five French decorations, two for gallantry, three for combat, and an acquaintance with the world denied to many twice his age.') Then he gave me a tip about locking my door behind me at all times.

'You've heard the old saying, "Honour among thieves . . ."' He winked. 'Well, it used to be true but not any longer.'

He left to rejoin the dinner queue and I continued setting the room aright until everyone was served and the corridor was clear. The target of many stares – suspicious, uncomprehending, curious or simply dull-eyed – I felt quite unlike a free man.

Sitting in my room towards evening, I could hear the sounds of keys rattling on the ends of chains, of doors being unlocked, opened, closed and locked again, accompanied by a 'Thank you' from the man who knows that tomorrow he will have to repeat his request another dozen times. The tea trolley rolled past the door and the smell of school dinners wafted underneath. Whispers, shouts, small snatches of conversation, reached me from the gathering congregation outside . . . 'Have you found out about it yet . . .', 'Did you see him for me . . .', 'legal aid', 'got nicked', 'my wife'. . . .

The crowd thickened, was fed and slowly dispersed for lock-up between five and six.

Suddenly the corridors are empty, the men behind bars, locked up. Along the landings the duty officers parade, locking one cell door after another, until everything is closed and total silence reigns. This silence spreads on several occasions every day, each time the eerie lock-up ritual is performed, transforming the busy hubbub into a wilderness: after breakfast, after dinner, after tea, and again at bedtime.

The disappearance of the prisoners from the floor of the prison never ceased to affect me; it was like the sudden disintegration of flesh from the skeleton. I hardly ever stayed in the prison during the lock-up periods, feeling – absurdly – most vulnerable then, without the warmth of surrounding bodies and voices.

Without the presence of the faces which give it life, the rigid principles governing the organization of the prison surface and become apparent again: encoded in the insistence upon routine – the routine of routines, never, never changing – certified by the apparatus of confinement, proclaimed, even, by the architecture.

It seems at first labyrinthine: branches stemming in every direction, housing nests of activity and life; through the metal gate to the right of my room was, on the one side – past another metal gate – the kitchen, beyond it the storeroom; on the other side the clothing store and then, through a gate and up some stairs, the education department. Directly facing my room were double wooden doors leading to the gym and, beyond, the exercise yard; down the corridor to the left of me you came upon the central hub of the prison where the wings crossed and the effect was like that of looking down long avenues in a strange city.

If one could sit on a rooftop above the prison, overlooking the sloping roofs of the four wings which make up the main body, crowned by a fenestrated hexagonal dome over the hub, with the subsidiary buildings dotted around, all wrapped up in the wall, it would seem to have a resemblance to a very large factory, or one of northern England's nineteenth-century mills – only larger, more extensive, than any mill. What would set it apart from the mill most noticeably would be its silence.

When I was outside the prison – after running the exhausting gauntlet of four gates, which I never ceased to dread – I hurried to get away. I thought:

There will never be a time when I am not relieved to be out of this place. I was wrong. But on that first night I felt exhilarated, lucky; buying a newspaper and reading it over a pint of beer seemed a privilege, so did keeping an appointment with a friend; choosing something for dinner, running for a train – these felt like magnificently healthy actions.

In a prison community, as in any other, a subtle network of connections is in the constant process of being forged, binding the citizens together through the establishment of a set of distinct customs and codes. In a prison these social guidelines are more rigid and inflexible than in other communities, which, for some, makes it a matter of urgency to escape them; but for others they may be correspondingly difficult to breach. 'My greatest fear', wrote one prisoner during the course of a class exercise designed to elicit spontaneous responses to simple questions, 'is that one day they will open the gates of this prison and kick me out.'

This is one form of gate fever; more commonly, gate fever is the fear which takes hold about a month before the prisoner is due to be released, during which, time – abnormally slow in passing even at best – begins to drag tortuously, and all manner of impediments to the arrival of freedom are suddenly conceivable: bureaucratic error, the revival of some ancient, unanswered crime, an unpaid fine, death, or simply a newly discovered, irresistible waning of the desperate hunger to be released.

This is the inside-out reaction to prison, perverse but in some ways appropriate because prison is an inside-out world, governed by its own laws and assumptions, with walls designed not to keep aliens out but to hold the citizens in; without a flag or a president or votes or taxes or official stratification – except of prisoners and prison officers; the city, as Victor Serge wrote, 'at once besieged and dominated by the enemy within'. The leader of this city is seen by his own citizens as a tyrant and, if he exercises his tyranny effectively, by strangers as a good man. The society is undeniably cruel, yet one of its alleged purposes is to fit men for a better one. As a repository of misery and shame, it strives for perfectability. Its code cannot admit individuality, yet when the gate is finally opened on the world where inside is assumed to be in and outside out, it boasts of despatching a person of strengthened character. Given the unresolvable nature of these contradictions, it is hardly surprising that some citizens prefer to stay put.

There are other forms of gate fever – pervasive and perennial symptoms of confinement. If I had one conspicuous intention upon entering this forgotten city – and in some ways I wished to go, like any good traveller going to a foreign place, without intentions and without preconceptions – it was to listen to the voice and the interplay of voices, to what was said about imprisonment and how it was said.

'Stick around,' prisoners and prison officers alike told me knowingly, 'you'll see some things.' They were right, even though the things were often scattered across long tedious gaps in the days, in the weeks, when nothing happened, not even the exchange of gossip. This austere climate leads some people into madness; out of it, however, is forced not only the paranoia which threatens life, but also the sensitivity – one of the most impressive sights in the prison – which insists on celebrating it.

2 The Body (I)

Curious to discover something about the ancestors of the men I would be meeting in the prison, I scoured the local library and the East Sussex Record Office for evidence, and enquired in the prison itself; but little exists to characterize the men (and women) who were the first inhabitants of the New Prison.

A senior officer showed me a collection of glass slides from the turn of the century: primitive mug shots, of shaven-headed or bowler-hatted men with coarse faces, dressed in thick, arrow-patterned suits, and others of pock-marked, prematurely aged, bonneted women. Joseph Lawrence, 1901, no. 1542: a wall-eyed old man with a thick beard. J. Chuter, 1905, no. L543: shaven-headed, a look of defiance in his eyes. Anna Bailey, young and almost pretty; Mary Evans, vacant, with a down-turned mouth . . . . The slide tells us nothing of where they came from, how they spoke, what they had done or were capable of doing; like today's mug shots, their effect is to disguise, not identify, the sitter.

A prison Chaplain's notebook from the years 1842–3 (referring to duties performed in the old prison) was of a little more help. It contained copies of letters written by women on behalf of themselves or their sons, poems and verse-letters by prisoners, and the following note from one prisoner to another written in blood with a piece of hard cheese rind:

> I hope you will get off with twelve months. Send me word how you was nailed and how you came to be nailed and how came your old woman to be nailed and what street you lived in. I was living in quite a square street. I never associated with any of the thieves. I had been in – [Lewes?] nearly 12 months and Solomon said he did not know I was in the town. I always took my things to London to sell. It was against my will that that tea-caddy was offered for sale. It was my old woman's fault. She said she knew it was all right, she had known the woman for five years and had sold her things before.

The Chaplain himself was a man of dull perception, firmly of the belief that the road to reform led through punishment. With satisfaction, he recorded instances of prisoners being brought to their senses (and to prayer, which was the same thing) after a thorough flogging or a spell in the dark cell or on restricted diet. His written entries do nothing at all to bring to life his charges – it is left to themselves to do that, in their letters – but he did record the difficulty which warders had, in these days of enforced silence, in keeping prisoners from communicating with one another.

One woman and her man had quite a language of their own by coughing only and in chapel used to carry on a regular conversation in this way. Among the London pickpockets there was a complete code by signal. They would find out, without an officer being able to detect, or without uttering a word, the whole particulars of each other's cases. They told their sentences by placing so many fingers on the mouth, which meant months, or on the ears for years and had other signs I could never fathom and the meanings of which they carefully guarded.

Although the conditions governing it have since changed, in that silence is no longer enforced, the tradition of private codes and signals of communication among prisoners remains, for example in prison slang.

In the Public Record Office, where I read the Chaplain's notebook, I found in the local paper the familiar reports of mid-nineteenth-century rough justice: in August 1856 Ann Weller, a prostitute, appeared before the judge in Lewes charged with stealing a sheet from the Globe Inn, which she sold for a shilling. She received two months' hard labour and was not allowed expenses. On the same day, Charles Robinson was given a month's hard labour for being drunk.

It was here too that I stumbled across the report of the execution of John Murdock – alias 'Joseph Williams' – in a copy of the *Sussex Express*, dated 9 August 1856. I was immediately impressed by the reporter's literary skill. He captures the quick of his subject, portraying him as a man alive – though ironically, of course, it took the divestment of his life on the scaffold to inspire such empathy.

Nineteen years old and illiterate, Murdock, a former seaman, killed a jailer while trying to escape from Hastings Jail where he was awaiting trial on a charge of pickpocketing. His take, in George Street, Hastings, was 3½d.

Murdock put his arms round the jailer's neck and, depriving him of the use of his legs by pushing his own knee into the man's knee joint, strangled him. It was, commented the *Express*, 'garotting in its worst form'.

The jury and some inhabitants of Lewes made efforts to have the sentence commuted to a term of imprisonment, or transportation, but it is unlikely that Murdock was much lamented by his fellow prisoners, for it emerged that as well as being a thief he was a police informer, and was even suspected of having led others into crime in order to gain the 'conviction money'.

This revelation was made by Murdock's stepfather in an eleventh-hour plea to the Secretary of State. He blamed the police for the young man's predicament, arguing that if Murdock's services had not been sought by them – more than one policeman stated that 'he was the best scout they ever had', the stepfather boasted proudly – then he would have been out of harm's way, at sea.

As a final attempt to gain authoritative support for their son, the parents looked to a plain-clothes policeman who had assured them that he would be present at the trial, 'and speak to his known humanity'; instead of which, the letter plaintively concludes, 'he obtained leave to absent himself, and did not return until after his trial was over'.

No one else had any interest in the condemned man in Lewes Prison except the hangman, William Calcraft, who had the job of converting him into a lifeless body, and the large crowd which turned out to witness the rare spectacle.

The power of fascination it held for them was caught in the account of the hanging and its preliminaries printed in the *Express*:

As the time approached when he was to suffer, he frequently exhibited the utmost mental agony and wept bitterly. He slept three hours on Monday night and rose early, but took no breakfast, the only thing of which he partook during the morning being a half-pint of porter. From this, and from the utter prostration which he had exhibited, it was feared that some difficulty would be experienced in getting him to the place of execution; that however was not the case.

About half-past eleven he expressed a strong request to be allowed to see the boy Wright who was present when he committed the crime. The request was complied with and the lad was brought to him. Murdock addressed him most fervently, and urged him in the strongest and most affectionate terms to take warning by him; but we regret to say the youth, who is only about 12 years of age, evinced but little feeling and appeared to treat in a very light manner the solemn interview in which he was taking so prominent a part.

The scaffold was erected just inside the centre of the eastern wall, and from an early hour on Monday evening a few people of the lowest character continued to come in from the Brighton road, and remained in the vicinity of the gaol up to the time of the execution, and as the morning advanced others came in; the arrivals by train were very small and at the time of the execution there were not 1,000 persons present of all classes, and only a very few had pretensions to respectability. A party of police were stationed round the gaol during the whole of the previous night under the charge of inspector Daws, and in the morning the force was considerably augmented, several of the men being in plain clothes. But their services were not required, the mob being probably the most orderly that ever assembled at an execution.

Shortly before 12 the prison bell was tolled, but was not heard outside the walls. Mr Sanders (the governor), Mr C. Palmer (the sheriff's agent), and the Rev. R. Burnett (the chaplain), visited the prisoner in his cell. He said he had been well treated while in confinement, and when bidding farewell to the governors, chaplain and warders thanked them for the kindness they had exhibited towards him. Calcraft, having entered, proceeded to pinion the prisoner's hands, and the procession was then formed and proceeded to the scaffold. . . . On arriving at the foot of the scaffold, the prisoner ascended the ladder first, and on reaching the top he walked to the centre of the platform with a slow tremulous step. He appeared perfectly resigned, indeed one would scarcely have expected to see a stout-built young man of 19, who had been hardened as it were to crime so completely passive and inanimate. He had evidently been in tears recently, and shook visibly. The chaplain and other officers followed him on to the scaffold immediately, and the rev. gentleman proceeded to read the solemn service for the dead, while Calcraft put the prisoner under the drop, and placed the white cap over his head. He wore the same dress as when on his trial, and his shirt front was open to enable the executioner to adjust the fatal noose. This he did in a few seconds, and then flung the other end of the rope over the beam, and made a running knot after which he went below. The poor wretch now shook violently, and opened and closed his hands in a convulsive manner. He could scarcely stand, and moved to and fro, exclaiming in a low and fervent tone 'Pray for my poor father and mother.' 'Lord Jesus, receive my spirit!' The next instant the bolt was withdrawn and he fell through the trap. The jerk apparently deprived him of sensibility, if not of life, for he appeared to die almost without a struggle. After hanging about an hour the body was cut down and buried within the precincts of the prison.

In this report the life in the body is apparent, in some hopeless way, and the voice, which is always missing in minute books and official reports, is audible.

3 The Body (II)

The prim officialese of prison parlance – 'inmate', 'segregation unit', 'cellular confinement', 'placed on report' – is not intended to describe the true nature of the prisoner's world; if anything, it purposely evades it. Inside the gate, terms like these constitute a tidy fiction, generally ignored though always available to project a sense of order and propriety, to impress the dignitary or visitor who has not learned the nature of prison ventriloquism.

At other times inmates are cons and prison officers are screws; the word for a sentence is bird, probably a product of Cockney rhyming slang – birdlime (a sticky substance for catching birds): time – although the image that registers in the mind is of a bird in a cage. A cell is a peter, from the lock manufacturer, Peter Chubb (the same word, from a previous world, is used for a safe). The prison itself is the nick, which in different parts of the wood means both to steal and to arrest, and also echoes Old Nick, the Devil. When a cell is raided it's a spin and the screws involved are burglars. A ghosting is when a con is moved out of the nick without warning, and the ghost train usually has several screws on board, sometimes dressed for action in MUFTI gear. A bad screw is a dog and time spent in segregation – the block – where the worst dogs often are, is chokey.

Some of the current prison vocabulary is simple rhyming slang, with relevance only to those inside – jam roll: parole, for example; the origin of other parts is easy to trace: puff, snout, hooch, firm; of others, less so: a nonce, a lag, a grass, to blank, kyting. (Sex offender, experienced convict, informer, to ignore, passing fraudulent cheques.)

For the prisoner these words are one of many ways of escape, forged by generations of men in prison cells in order to steal a mouthful of the freedom which language bestows. Slang is verbal rebellion, its aim is to subvert official terminology and, therefore, the official way of perceiving the world. The real reason for calling a cell a peter is to take the power of possession out of the hands of the screw and place it in those of the con.

Only one such potent word did I ever hear coming from the other side of the uniform: the word was *body*, the system's off-the-record way of describing its charge.

When I first heard the term used in this way – by an Assistant Governor speaking on the telephone to the leader of an escort party taking prisoners to London the next day: 'I'll have the bodies ready for you' – it gave me a shock. I was affected perhaps a little by its crudeness, but all the more so because it struck me as such an appropriate description of a certain way of behaving, which gradually becomes a way of being, induced in the prisoner. To become a docile body – without wishes, desires, needs, choices or rights – is the fate the system has in store for him.

All bodies pass through Reception, regardless of whether they have arrived (in the 'meat wagon') from court, from the police cells or from another prison.

To the outsider the reception block is not a particularly unpleasant or intimidating place. It consists of a set of rooms – holding room for new arrivals, kitchen, bathroom, lavatories – with the main office situated in the centre. The orderlies (all of whom are prisoners) know that their jobs, which get them out of lock-up periods as well as bringing other perks such as coffee and real milk, are among the best in the prison and they cooperate efficiently with the prison officers, who in turn treat them with the civility which good management displays towards its workers.

In a room adjoining the office a television set is on constantly and in the summer months the orderlies can watch cricket and tennis during the idle moments between fetching cups of tea and kit for new arrivals. Upstairs is the property room, where prisoners' belongings are stored in cardboard boxes bearing name and number, stacked on metal shelves, and next door a small room contains the camera and chair required for the taking of official photographs.

The officers are engaged in constant chatter, answering telephones and bantering with the orderlies; this close atmosphere itself contributes to the feeling of exclusion which the new prisoner has when he enters the block to begin the reception ceremony.

Gavin Price came from Horsham Magistrate's Court. He was handcuffed when he stepped inside, a policeman before and behind him, but the handcuffs were taken off when he was placed in the small waiting room.

Gavin Price was thirty years old, with red hair in loose curls (possibly the vestiges of a perm), red-rimmed eyes and pointed features which stopped just short of being handsome. He carried a few things with him, suggesting that he had gone to court that morning knowing he would be remanded in custody: three worn paperback novels (a Len Deighton, an Alistair

MacLean and one other), toothpaste and shampoo, tobacco, papers, a lighter, flints and a box of matches. He was wearing a thick pullover but no jacket, although it was winter, and had £1.11 in his pocket. Sitting in the waiting room with another – a slight, ageing man remanded on a charge of having had intercourse with a twelve-year-old girl – he did not appear worried or frightened, but in his look of determined patience there was a tense eagerness to have the ritual over and done with.

Telephones were ringing, jokes were passed to and fro, cups of tea or coffee were ordered or offered. Here, in the main reception room, it was all routine, with no sense of crisis, trouble or shame. This prisoner was no different, in their eyes, from the one before or the one who would be coming after him. In the first few days of this week alone there had been twenty-five new arrivals so far.

The prison officers talked casually and laughed among themselves – not callously but in such a way as to separate them from their charges. In an hour they would have handed over to the next shift and be gone, into the pub or back in front of the television with their wives and children. It was an easy assumption of power.

Gavin Price was brought in and placed in a dog box, one of a row of cubicles facing the officers' desks, where he sat silently, with his head down.

After arranging the various sheets of paper and files on his desk, Principal Officer Robson called the prisoner over to stand before him. The charge was deception: passing dud cheques, or kyting. He was due to appear in court again in a week's time, when he might be given bail – though, since he had already been refused it, it seemed unlikely unless his counsel could produce a good reason in the meantime – or he might stay for several months in F Wing, the adult remand wing where he was headed now, until his trial. (Men on more serious charges are often remanded for a year or more.)

PO Robson began to fill out the warrant:

Name: Gavin Price
Date of birth: 2.3.54
Ethnic group: White
Religion: C of E
Address: 71, N – Street, Horsham.

To this was added the information that he had been remanded in custody by the magistrate's court and that he was unconvicted. Then PO Robson looked up at the small blackboard hanging on the wall which shows the latest number ready to be reissued, handed down from someone released that day, and allocated it to Price: N68965. . . . From the moment when he is christened with this number he becomes a code in the system.

Next the Principal Officer telephoned the hospital and asked for a member of the medical staff to come over to Reception and give the prisoner a medical examination; N68965 was told to sit in the dog box again, until the medical officer arrived.

The examination took a cursory form.

'Is there anything wrong with you?'

'I'm asthmatic.'

'How long have you been asthmatic?'

'About twenty years.'

'Anything else?'

'Don't think so.'

'Take drugs?'

'No.'

'Not suicidal?'

'No.'

'Subject to fits?'

'No.'

'Haven't seen a psychiatrist lately?'

A shrug and, for the first time, the suggestion of a laugh.

'No.'

The medical officer then told him that he would be subject to a proper examination in the morning and sent him back to the main reception area where he was interviewed on aspects of his personal history, in a more mundane sense, by another officer. This one wanted to know if Price had served any previous custodial sentences. He had.

'When was the last one?'

'Two and a half years ago.'

'Where?'

'Barlinnie, Glasgow.'

'For how long?'

'Nine months.'

'What for?'

'Deception.' The prison officer looked up, widened his eyes, and again that half-laugh was drawn from Price. His date of release from Barlinnie was noted and then he was measured, weighed, and examined for identifying marks. There was a tattoo on each forearm – professional, not prison jobs – of a globe with a circular scroll containing the names Charlotte, on the left, and, on the right, Mother.

The officer finished with him.

'Are you ready for this one yet?' he asked the officer who was to deal with him next. The prisoner, standing two feet away, is conscious of the impersonal reference. The next officer, copying from notes into a file, replied that he was not quite ready and Price was told to sit once more in one of the five dog boxes. He took up his position like a man in a railway waiting room made for one. A reception orderly asked him if he would like a cup of tea. Price, brightening, expecting to be served with it, answered that he would. The orderly simply pointed to a tray of cups and told him where the urn was. But he did bring him a piece of toast with cheese on it, which Price ate half of. After another ten minutes of waiting, the officer cleared his desk and summoned him.

'Right.'

Price stood up and walked over to the desk. This officer filled out a property card. Some people, particularly if they are of no fixed abode, bring a lot of property into prison with them. It is stored and returned when the man leaves. This prisoner, however, had very little.

The officer counted out the £1.11 in front of him, made a record of it and put it into a cash drawer. The shampoo and toothpaste, he explained, were prohibited, as they might be laced with drugs or poison. They were thrown in a bin. The same prohibition applied to the matches and the packet of tobacco which had been opened. However, when Price objected that it had been sealed until being searched in the police cells, the prison officer gave him the benefit of the doubt and let him keep his tobacco. He could also keep his lighter but not the flints. The officer then informed him that as a remand prisoner he would be allowed to have money and a cooked meal with a pint of beer or a half bottle of fortified wine sent in each day. To all these instructions, rules, privileges and prohibitions, Price mulishly acquiesced.

Next he was sent for a shower – the new prisoner's baptism – and on returning was given bedding (clean sheets but not clean blankets) and then instructed to follow another officer through a door which led directly from Reception to F Wing. From the wing office there he was designated a cell which he would share, for however long it took for him to be sentenced or acquitted, with a partner he had never met.

As reception procedure is a duty for the authorities, it is a ritual to be suffered by the prisoner. It is also the prison gate abstracted and stretched through time. For as much as he feels that this ordeal is trying and humiliating ('Are you ready for this one?'), yet he knows it is a form of life which belongs in the world he has just left. People are sitting behind desks, not locked in prison cells, or parading prison landings; they offer you cups of tea and treat you in a way that is similar, if only on the surface, to the way that you are treated in many other situations – being interviewed for a job, signing on for work (or on the dole), seeing the doctor. All that is part of life and all of it is stopping after the end of this ceremony.

From now on everything about N68965 will be conditioned by his confinement, which is suddenly the most prominent thing in his existence: what the body sees, smells, touches, hears; who he speaks to and his range of address. He is already deprived of his home and his freedom of movement and, if he is convicted, to that list will be added money, clothes, voting rights, responsibility for all financial affairs (including those of his family), his sexual needs and choices, even his contact with the natural world. A man might go for twenty years without seeing a flower or smelling grass. There are no children in the prison and no animals, and, of course, no women. Apart from routine exercises in prison workshops, charity work or arts and crafts courses, he is deprived – perhaps most importantly of all – of his instinct to create.

From the day he is convicted, his daily routine will follow roughly this pattern: rise at 6.45 a.m., wash and slop out, then queue for breakfast. After eating breakfast locked in his cell, he starts work at eight, returns at 11.00, and is served dinner from the hot-plate at 11.20. He eats again in his cell and is locked up between 11.45 and one o'clock. There is no dining room here. Since mealtimes are followed by lock-up – during which the majority of prison officers take their break – every bite of prison food is eaten in silence.

From 1 to 2 p.m. there is gym for those who can make it. Those who can't, because of work or a visit, usually go in the morning, or else following the afternoon work session. All prisoners are returned to the wing by four o'clock, tea is served at 4.20 and they are locked up between 4.45 and six o'clock. Afterwards there is 'association' (except on Fridays) when prisoners can watch television, attend classes in the education unit, play snooker, table tennis or chess, read a book or listen to music. At 8.30 p.m. it is the end of one more day.

The next time I saw N68965 I did not recognize him. At least, I saw a face I recognized but I had difficulty in placing it. For a moment I thought I had seen someone I knew from outside, though I couldn't say who it was. He descended the metal steps which connect the landings in B Wing, nodded and half-smiled at me, then turned and walked away.

Three weeks had gone by. After another appearance in court and refusal of bail, Gavin Price changed his plea from not guilty to guilty and was sentenced to two years' imprisonment on four counts of deception. As he lived locally and the sentence was a comparatively light one, not involving a period of assessment in a large London prison, he was admitted back into Lewes. After a renewed reception procedure, he had been issued with a complete kit and housed in a cell on his own in C Wing.

The prison kit: two shirts, two pairs of underpants, one T-shirt, two vests, three pairs of socks, one pullover, one pair of grey trousers, one pair of jeans, one denim jacket, one pair of slippers, one pair of shoes, plus one gym vest, a pair of gym shorts and gym shoes, and two towels. The kit is passed down from man to man, so that when the newly admitted prisoner takes a shirt and puts it on, he is wearing something whose texture is already imbued with the tinge of confinement. The clothes do not fit properly, and they always belong to the prison. He is merely hired out to them for the duration of his stay, after which another will be assigned to them.

It was this clothing – blue-and-white striped shirt and grey flannels – which had brought about the difference in Price's appearance and made it difficult for me to recognize him, because formerly, as a remand prisoner, he had been allowed to wear his own clothes. The outfit is referred to as 'prison grey', although the jeans and T-shirt are blue and the shirt is blue-striped. Grey suits its mood and suits the weather of prison, and avoids the connotations which blue has in connection with prison officers and policemen.

Not only does this grey impose a uniformity upon prisoners, it alters their appearances by rearranging them structurally.

The change of personality which man in general undergoes when he becomes man-in-prison is illustrated by the photographs which prisoners keep in their cells, showing them as they were in their former lives. Almost invariably, they show an unrecognizable character dressed in, for example, white shirt, tweed jacket, tie, etc.

The photograph shows a group of men sitting round a dinner table, all looking at the camera. None of them seems familiar. He stands up and points to someone on the left-hand side of the table, smiling for the photographer. 'That's me,' he says.

It comes as a shock, this first recognition that the body had a former life and a former shape.

If compared side by side with the photograph which is taken of him when he first enters prison as a convict – the mug shot – the two snaps would display entirely different faces. The mug shot produces an act of defiance and as a result is virtually useless as a means of identifying someone. It portrays a face quite unlike that of the man it is supposed to represent: only the coincidence of numbers connects the two. People in certain societies forbid the camera to be pointed at them. Fearing it will capture their souls, they hide their faces from it. The prisoner cannot shun the camera deliberately in such a way, but he shields himself none the less, so the image that results is that of a mere body.

Every day the prisoner lives out the identity of the body, resisting it at the same time. Every day he considers the apartheid which is enforced between man in general and man-in-prison. In the eyes of the system which contains him, the former does not exist; to himself, the latter is a mere figment of the system itself, a failure of perception. However, it is in his interests not to stress this fact. So, time after time, moment by moment, maybe for years on end, he maintains a precipitous balancing act between how he sees himself and how he is seen by 'them'. If he sways too far one way and refuses to speak, to be seen and treated as a body, then the state has the right to bring its full power down on his head, ultimately to kill him. If, on the other hand, he leans too heavily in the opposite direction, then he is in danger of forfeiting the one precious thing he kept when he entered prison.

4 The Voice (I): An Innocent

Miller Steele was a young New Zealander serving two years for drug smuggling. He claimed to be innocent of this charge. A lot of people in prisons protest their innocence – indeed it has become a joke among prisoners themselves that 'prisons are full of innocent men'. But I believed Miller.

The case involved him accepting a television set from customs officers who, aware of its contents, delivered it to the house where Miller was living. The house was multi-occupant and the name on the large parcel was not his, but he accepted it anyway. He unwrapped it to make it fit through the front door of the house (the prosecution witnesses agreed that it was too large to get through without doing so) and left it, otherwise untouched, on the landing outside his room, until the owner was found.

Then he left the house. When he came back he shifted the television into his room for safety, at which point the customs officers, who had been tracking his movements since delivering the set, now abetted by police, swooped down on him. They opened the set and showed Miller the contents: thirteen pounds of good-quality marijuana. On the mantelpiece they found letters, written by his wife but signed, in an affectionate way, on behalf of both of them, which alluded to hashish – not marijuana, though the judge and jury failed to grasp the distinction – and making a connection to gain a personal supply.

These letters secured his downfall. Like many other people, Miller and his wife enjoyed a smoke from time to time, but it is extremely doubtful that he had anything to do with a television set packed with grass, arriving from a country whose name he could hardly pronounce and which he could not have found on a map.

He had no criminal record and nothing in his background to prepare him for prison.

'I was quite bewildered, really. I was in police cells for two nights and all the time I was expecting them to come and let me out and they sort of led me to believe that, but in the end I came here instead. I was in a van, cuffed up with two other people: two together, your left hands are cuffed up right from the court, the holding cells in the court, until you're brought here. You don't really know what's going on, you're just following the bloke in front. They ask you some questions: have you ever been in prison before? Have you any money? Who do we contact? Your religion, and so on. They process you and give you a prison number. You have to have a shower and you have to have a meal when you come in in the evenings; the normal prison sort of food, mashed potatoes, peas and pie, something like that, a bit of bread maybe. I was just loathing, all loathing.

All the time I was here, on remand, I was always expecting someone to come and say it's all been a terrible mistake, you can go. I was always waiting for that but it never happened.

There were two YPs on the bus with me and they were chatting away about how they were hiding cigarettes in their underpants to have a smoke in the cells, you know, they were old hands even though they were kids. They were really jovial – a lot of people are jovial, most people. You don't see many sad faces in Reception, just the newcomers.

Anyway, when they gave us our bedding and took us through to the wing, the first thing I associated it with was that *Porridge*, that TV series. I didn't know what to expect. It was antiquated, as if it was out of the Victorian times, or out of the movies. The movies was the only thing I had to go by: I expected homosexuality, junkies, God knows what. I thought I could look after myself just by keeping out of the way. I was expecting it, but it wasn't too bad. I was just given a cell number and asked about my diet, and then I was put in a cell with another guy. As it turned out the other guy was someone I got on well with, he was a good chap. He'd done two or three prison sentences before, he was about four or five years older than me, but he had travelled a lot as well, so we had a little bit in common. And he was quite a clean person, had some self-respect. It's important, I believe, to keep some sort of self-respect; like when I saw that you had to piss in a bucket I was disgusted. In the time I've been here I've used it maybe half a dozen times. And if you have to shit between 8.30 p.m. and 7 a.m. then you have to shit in the bucket too, or shit in a newspaper and throw it out of the window.

Visits from my wife are the most important thing to me. You get three visits a month, lasting for two hours. It's always my wife. Once my sister came with my wife and once a good friend of my wife and myself came, but other than that it's always my wife. Two hours three times a month; you haven't really got a lot.

I look forward to the next visit as soon as the last one's over. I'm always anxious, because it's some peace. You're with the person you're most comfortable with. I come over to the wing and have a wash and a shave and whatnot and change clothes. I'm always tense. I always get a lift from the visit unless my wife's unhappy, then I get depressed. You're helpless.

I wish I could think of nothing a lot of the time, but it's hard because you've got too much time. You sit there and work yourself into a depression. Then I read a book or listen to a tape or something. You have to push yourself to do things. Even like some days I don't feel like going to the gym but I always push myself because you have to have something to occupy yourself. I feel that everyone has to have a bit of discipline in prison. But sometimes I feel that if I discipline myself so much that I can stop worrying – about my wife, for example – it'll be like letting go. I remember when I first came in, I was on the cleaners and the work is just about an hour a day, so the rest of the time I used to lie there and think about things and write letters. At that stage I was feeling as close to my wife as if I was still out there. And then when I went to Reception to work, I was so busy all the time that I was too busy to think about it, and it felt like I was being taken away from her.'

5 The Cell

All of my meetings had so far taken place in my own cell. A senior member of staff had advised me that the bores and liars would come first, and he was right. Bores, liars and worse, hard to get rid of and tightening the claustrophobia in the tiny room.

A Czechoslovakian intellectual insisted on reading me his latest epistle to the Home Secretary, packed with references to and quotations from Plato, St Augustine, Schopenhauer, Nietzsche, Freud and a score of other big names. It took an hour. I tried not to look bored as he paused to roll another cigarette and said there were only eleven pages to go.

'Think about it,' he said as he left. I did. It made no sense.

An Englishman described in long and tender detail his part in a bank fraud in Switzerland involving £139,000. Interesting, I thought. From there he went on to his garage which specialized in Rolls-Royces, his wine bar in Marylebone, his business partner's 'very close relationship' with King Hussein, his Oxford education, his family home in Scotland where the back garden was 'big enough for a grouse shoot', another family estate on the south-east coast, the hotel he had bid for in Ireland – 'only £37,000 short' – his massive tax problems (implying massive assets), solicitors' charges, law suits for and against, investments, house in New Jersey, 'strong box' in Toronto; and a final piece of advice – 'Never talk business with friends.'

He was serving a short sentence for theft of less than £300, information he released grudgingly.

'When's this book of yours coming out?' a boyish chap with shining eyes and a black goatee beard asked. I explained that it would take some time.

'Well, if you can hang on for a bit it might appear at the same time as mine.'

'What's that about?'

'It's called *I Am God*.'

A few weeks later someone threw a lighted torch into his cell and both culprit and victim were ghosted out within hours.

'Burning out' and 'turning over' cells were familiar disturbances, forms of vicarious assault and self-mutilation. The cell is where the prisoner spends most of his time, does his waiting, is most himself. It is the place where he sleeps, eats, writes, reads, fantasizes and masturbates, shits and pisses, reaches despair and rescues himself (if he does rescue himself: it is also, inevitably, the place where suicides occur). The pain of frustration produces feelings which invade the mind and body, which are finally unbearable. Then he has four alternatives: to take it out on a screw, on another prisoner, on himself, or on the cell, which is like a second self.

There are eighteen cells on each side of every landing and, in C Wing, four landings: C1, C2, C3, and C4, the last three known by everyone as the twos, the threes and the fours. The twos is the ground level; C1, which is below ground, is reserved for 'sections', convicted prisoners awaiting sentence. They, like the remands, are not permitted to mix with or talk to the serving men, who therefore possess a special status within this prison which holds several different kinds of prisoner: they are at once the brahmins – the elite – and the untouchables.

To walk through the silent combs after lock-up, seeing only the identical doors of the facing rows of cells, you might think that every cell was alike, and that every landing had the same atmosphere. In fact, no two cells are even similar – except the very basest, and even then squalor reflects the face of its creator – and each of the three landings has a different climate.

Take the cells. The anonymous blue doors offer no clue to who lives inside or what goes on; all that the door has to tell is written on the cell card slotted between brackets on the outside: surname, number, religion and length of sentence. Every cell has a judas hole – a traitor to the prisoner. If you looked through all eighteen on your way from one end of the landing to the other, you would find a different scene in each.

Like people in furnished rooms, prisoners usually decorate their cells and rearrange the furniture after moving in, accumulating bits and pieces from other cells when the occupants leave, or else by exchange; a set of cupboards, for example, for an extra table, or a chair for a poster. So when a prisoner invites you into his cell he is asking you into his home, and the same traditional ceremonies of hospitality prevail. In this set of cages, hospitality is one of the surprises. It is the hospitality traditionally shown by the poor towards strangers. Always be pleased to give. Before I could offer a cigarette, I would be offered one; the same with coffee, records, books – take this, take that. And when somebody borrowed something of mine, the principle worked in reverse: it was returned punctiliously and with thanks.

Dan has virtually no furniture in his cell, but is obsessive about keeping it clean. Ron has a full noticeboard of pictures of his beautiful wife and daughter; the daughter, it turns out, is not really Ron's, although it isn't he who tells you this, but the knowledge gives the cell a different atmosphere next time you enter. James has recently discovered art and his walls are covered with reproductions of paintings from the Italian Renaissance, plus a few of his boyfriend, still in another jail. Garry's – an ex-soldier – is ascetic and spartan, with the window open even in mid-winter.

Some cells are filthy and barren of everything except a bed with some twisted grey sheets strewn across it or on the floor, a chamberpot poking out from underneath and graffiti scarring the walls. In these I felt least comfortable but most moved. The surroundings spoke eloquently of the pass the man had reached, echoing his degradation, certifying his inability to prove to himself that there was even one decent thing about his existence.

In Kenny's cell, for example – potentially one of the most pleasant, at the far end of the threes, with a view which caught the Sussex Downs and some of the town rooftops uncontaminated by convict life – there was nothing but a broken radio besides the bed, table and chair. The bed was never made and a variety of putrefying foodstuffs usually littered the table. No doubt he now and then attempted to tidy it up, only to find, about an hour later, that it had mysteriously reverted to its former state. This was the cell's – and the owner's – condition.

Other cells could have been looked after by Dutch housekeepers, prim and neat, with a sterility imported to add to that which is already inherent in the cell design. Yet others were homely, with pictures on the walls and curtains at the barred window.

The regulations state that the prisoner is allowed a battery-operated radio, which most of them have; at the discretion of the governor, he may be permitted certain additional luxuries, such as, at Lewes, a record player and twelve records, or, in other prisons but not here, a portable television. The rules similarly state that the prisoner may keep six books in his cell, though this limit tends to be overlooked. For other extras, such as a typewriter, special permission must be sought and will only be granted if there is good reason.

A landing is like a street with the cells as its houses. People drop in to borrow a spoonful of sugar or to have a chat or a smoke. Entrance to certain cells is by invitation only, usually if there is hashish – 'puff' – on offer. But it is unwise to let a reputation for hospitality grow too grand, or else the burglars will pay a call.

Of the landings, the fours was the most fashionable, the lifers' landing.

The prisoners serving short sentences were housed on the twos. The homosexuals had a clique on B Wing threes; this was called the married quarters.

Billy Miles explained how most prisoners taped up the judas eye used to spy on them from the outside, and also how they wedged up their doors by digging a trough about two inches long just behind the door on the inside and fitting into it a piece of wood: if the burglars arrive, the wedge holds them back long enough for whatever needs stashing to be stashed or else dropped out of the window. The judas – 'the eye that never slept' – is now a slit, but once it was round, carved and painted to resemble a human eye.

Billy was the first person to invite me into his cell. When he came to see me he talked about the trouble he had got into inside prison, how his disciplinary record extended far beyond anyone else's. He talked about it with pride; it was his sole achievement. He kept himself to himself, he said, had only one real friend, with whom he played chess most evenings. He always had his bit of puff and more than once flipped off the lid of his tobacco tin to show me, stuck to the inside of the lid like a piece of chewing gum, the little wad of hash.

At first I was shy of taking up his invitation. I hadn't even been on the fours yet and the prospect of being swallowed up by a prison cell was exciting but also frightening. I wasn't ready yet to be so vulnerable.

'When are you coming up?' Billy would ask. 'Sunday?' And I would find some reason for not being in at the time he suggested on Sunday.

'Monday then.'

I never came in on Mondays at all. 'I'll let you know,' I would say.

Finally, conscious of offending him by rejecting his hospitality, I got up the courage and for the first time climbed the metal spiral staircase to the fours where I saw him watching the communal television. Resisting the stares of the others who surrounded him on the rows of seats before the screen, I tapped Billy's shoulder and immediately he stood up and beckoned me to follow him towards his cell, only a few yards away.

A hundred pairs of eyes seemed to follow us. What was going on? What was Billy going to get up to in there with that fellow? I realized that for the egregious Billy I was a status symbol, and also that it would do me no harm in the eyes of the suspicious to be seen being welcomed so readily into a cell on the fours.

Billy's cell had one outstanding feature: its walls were covered, floor to ceiling, in pornographic pictures.

''Scuse the photographs,' Billy said, selecting a record and placing it carefully on the player, 'they were here when I moved in and I just decided to leave them up.'

Most were of the sort commonly found in magazines on newsagents' shelves; one or two showed couples having intercourse or a woman performing fellatio on a man. Billy was oblivious to them; for him their allure had long faded. He offered me the most comfortable seat, on the bed, took the hard chair for himself, and gave me a choice between tea or coffee. I chose the latter and he made it from a flask of hot water while the music pounded out on to the landing.

Billy talked above the beat but his wallpaper preoccupied me. The images were distracting, certainly, but it also struck me as being peculiar that woman should be represented in this place in this way. In the photographs each woman was represented as being all sex, as if sexual desire and bounty were not only her essence but her everything. Sex was all there was to be known about her, nothing else. Here she was, legs spreadeagled, in a schoolgirl uniform, clutching a switch; in another she smiled in the act of undressing. She did not ask the viewer to see her in any other way.

The deepest, if not the most conspicuous, gap in prison is the space where sex ought to be. Five years, ten years, without a touch, without a kiss, without a cry, without so much as a look. 'I have never come into contact with another human being in almost twenty years', wrote Jack Henry Abbott, 'except in combat; in acts of struggle, of violence.'

Sex talk is mostly crude – or embarrassed, which amounts to the same thing – with a vocabulary and an attitude borrowed from the magazines out of which Billy's pictures came. Heterosexual activity is out of the question, and the channels through which sex influences day-to-day life on the outside – through dress, speech, visual and auditory sensations – are stopped up.

It appears to have been designed this way, the essentials of prison life being regulated to stem every desire before it reaches its fulfilment. No doubt this was once intended to be a part of the scheme of punishment, but it now conflicts, unignorably, with one of the modern system's professed aims, which is to rehabilitate its captives.

The prison homosexuals are often despised, yet they deserve respect for having sought to share their desire – if not always their feelings – with another life. As for the others, swaggering around in an atmosphere created solely by men, it was they who faced the danger of growing inverted.

Billy took another record from the rack, spread out several cigarette papers on the sleeve and gummed them together. He fingered some tobacco across the white sheet, produced a tack-head of hash from the lump in his tobacco tin, and began cooking it over the lighted match. Every night he did the same. He completed the rolling and got stoned once again.

'This', he said, holding up the skinny joint after the first draw and watching the smoke curl above his head, 'is what keeps the lid on the place.'

The first time I saw Simon he was standing in a straggled queue outside my door, waiting for the clothing store to open for the weekly kit change. One arm was crooked at a right angle in white plaster, and with it he gesticulated in the direction of the notice on my door.

'What's all this about, then?'

He wasn't smiling. He looked frightened and sounded frightened, as if even by asking the question he was risking himself. His head had recently been shaved and now was covered by a furze of cropped hair, and his skin was stretched tightly over his cheek and jaw bones. In his refusal to disguise his fear with a tough-guy act, it was possible to see the remnants of a fragile sensitivity, even tenderness.

I invited him in but he shook his head quickly, making at the same time a stiff movement with the plaster cast to signal No. So while we leaned against the door jambs, with other cons passing to and fro in the corridor, I explained why I was here and how I had got permission to wander freely within the prison walls, which amazed, or rather seemed to terrify, him most of all. Simon listened, saying little, nodding tensely. He had just come from a Category A dispersal prison (the larger, highly secure prisons where assessments are made) which, he said, had almost done for him, and now that he was here he was 'just trying to get my head back together'. He didn't trust the comparatively liberal regime here any more than he liked the severity of the place he had come from, and he didn't want any part of 'their mister-nice-guy games'. At times he seemed to be regarding the entire set-up as a snare designed solely to trap and destroy him. Moving him from the dispersal system to here, where the tempo was slower, was nothing more than the old hot-and-cold bath treatment used by torturers. He spoke about prison as if it were a purgatorial labyrinth stumbled into by mistake, from which one day soon he hoped to catch a glimpse of the light awaiting him. So no thanks, he wouldn't speak any more to me.

'I just want to wipe my mouth and get out of these places.' He raised his head a little, twisting his neck jerkily to the left, with his chin in the air.

When he did so his face resembled the hollowed-out turnip lanterns Scottish children used to carry on Halloween.

We kept on talking. He had served twelve years of a life sentence for the murder of a South African who had picked him up drunk from a pub in Hastings, taken him home in a taxi – 'I don't even remember getting out of the taxi'—and slept with him. When he woke up in the morning he got a bread knife from the kitchen and stabbed the sleeping seducer repeatedly.

That much he did remember and the jury found him guilty on a murder charge because he had the self-possession to go into the kitchen to choose the weapon.

'I would've got a manslaughter otherwise,' he said, 'been out of this place by now.'

How had he hurt his arm?

By punching his hand through a window in frustration after an argument with a screw.

'Windin' me up.' The skin tightened on the sharp cheekbones.

The worst thing of all was that it had stopped him painting. Painting was Simon's main interest. It was more than a hobby. It took up most of his spare time and he regarded it as his profession, by means of which he gained tobacco, dope, furnishings, real milk, even cash.

'Screws have bought my paintings,' he said. When he smiled his eyes stayed cold but his lips drew back across his teeth; somewhere along the line he had lost the art of smiling. I said that I would like to see some of his work. He seemed pleased and, speaking more evenly, promised to bring something down to show me next day. We made an appointment.

He left. He had eventually crossed the threshold into the room, though without sitting down, and I felt a small pride, as if through a tiny crack in the nightmare engulfing him I had been able to whisper a message, consisting perhaps of just a syllable, to another, deeper self.

The following day I was expecting him but he didn't turn up. When I saw him next, by accident again, this time at the noticeboard opposite the C Wing office, he said that he had changed his mind about talking to me – no offence, he just wanted to wipe his mouth and get out. More or less the same development unfolded as before, with me assuring Simon that I had no wish to make him do or say anything he didn't wish to, and with him relaxing slightly and gradually allowing himself a degree of trust.

It so happened that I had at home a new painting by my sister, Phyllis Davies, an artist. I told Simon about it and offered to bring it in next day to show him. He was enthusiastic about the suggestion and we parted, having made another appointment.

In the morning I had the painting with me. I propped it up on the shelf in my room. It was a large watercolour, with a foreground of bright yellow and lilac flowers, with two blue-grey tenement facades in the middle distance and a background of rooftops and gables affected by sunlight. It was full of colour.

I waited, but again he failed to turn up. This time I asked someone who I knew lived on the same landing to remind him, if they should happen to meet, of our arrangement and before the morning was out Simon appeared, apologizing for having 'forgotten'. He made straight for the painting, admiring it and passing critical comment. I reminded him of his offer to show me some of his own work. Sure, he said, of course. Why didn't he bring something down next afternoon? We arranged a time and he left.

When he stood me up for the third time I tried a different tactic. I went up the narrow spiral staircase to the fours and knocked on his door. You cannot actually produce much sound by knocking with the hand on the reinforced steel door of a cell: the method is to oblige the formality and call out. Simon was surprised to see me and suddenly embarrassed. He was again a different person, with a separate existence, from the one who had stood in front of the painting the day before and reflected its luminous surfaces. That sane, unclouded self was pursued by a much stronger double with a stronger voice which unbalanced the other before it ever gained a proper poise. The darkness of his confinement was heavier by far than the light secret he had discovered in art. Eventually, the balance might be shifted, but for the time being the daily struggle between the two selves was no contest.

He invited me in for a cup of coffee, closed the door and sat down. Then he stood up and opened it again and returned to his seat. Once more he got up to close it and this time dithered before he settled, finally, for having it half-open. He was talking all the time, startled into loquaciousness by the unexpected presence in his cell of a visitor in normal clothing, who had risen from a normal bed that morning and would go back to it, in safety, tonight.

Simon gave me the only chair and sat on the bed. He asked me what kind of music I liked. I saw a record by Marvin Gaye on the turntable and said that that would be fine. I kept the conversation on a simple track, ignoring his astonishment, steering it back to an everyday subject whenever there was a silence or a stare or a frightened comment such as, 'I can't believe this, you know, can't believe they let you come in here.'

Then he showed me some of his paintings. The plaster cast which had kept his painting arm at a right angle for the past six weeks had been removed and he had started working again. His proficiency was remarkable. There were Flemish landscapes, French still lifes, flower arrangements, sentimental postcards, pencil portraits (some commissioned by other prisoners, of a wife or a child) and others. On an easel at the foot of the bed was a canvas with the beginnings of what would, eventually, be an abstract in rather gaudy colours. Simon said that one was for a screw.

The technical expertise in his paintings was high – the detail was painted in with a Renaissance particularity – but all of his work was copied. There was scarcely an instance of the painter's individual vision in everything that he laid before me. Next to the painting of a child dabbling its feet in a pool was a postcard of the same scene.

I admired the paintings but their imaginative barrenness perturbed me. It was more than just a lack; rather, it was as if the infertility was the subject itself. If to paint is to escape, then Simon had forsworn his release.

This is not to say that he had no imagination. Its evidence was in fact in plentiful supply, but directed to a different purpose. His cell windows and bars had been blocked out completely by a pair of shutters made from cardboard on which were painted wooden slats and their shadows. Above them was an undulating cardboard pelmet, also made to look like wood. He had fashioned cardboard cupboards to keep coffee, tea and milk, and cardboard shelves held in place by skilfully cut cardboard brackets.

But the *tour de force* was a painting on the cork noticeboard which is affixed to the wall of every cell. It was started in order to hide an ugly crack across the surface but had developed into an elaborate work of art. It portrayed a Dutch landscape, with skaters on a frozen pond beneath a winter sky, lopsided houses, a windmill in the background, and a horse and some figures on the banks of the pond. On either side of the scene, Simon had draped curtains, to create the illusion of a splendid world seen through the window.

6 Maps

The first time I met him he was standing in the corridor where the meals were dished out, awaiting the arrival of the food trolleys. There were at least ten minutes to go before the hot-plate began serving but T.C. liked to be early. He was always the first or one of the first in the queue to be served and he took his meal back to his cell, ate it, and had the plate outside in the landing waiting to be collected before the mealtime lock-up. Any day he would be likely to knock on the door of my room at the end of the corridor to see if I happened to be free for a brief chat during the waiting time he always allowed before the barred gates to the kitchen were unlocked and the large trolleys rolled through.

Although I talked with him often in this fashion – about the books he was reading (Westerns), his prospects of release and his lack of family or friends – I never succeeded in travelling very far with T.C. I knew that he had served sixteen years of a life sentence for murder and was expecting to do at least four more. A year ago he had been scheduled for release and was transferred to an open prison; while there, however, he got involved in a scuffle with another prisoner, whereupon he was ghosted back to high security. Now, his prospect of an early release date was obscured. He was an embodiment of the contradiction in the philosophy of the prison service which places men in conditions of extreme pressure and then asks them to prove their fitness to return to a society where entirely different conditions obtain. If he breaks the rules, in confinement, he is judged unfit to live in freedom.

Pieces of hard information were distributed meanly throughout a vast spread of words, for T.C., once he started talking, was hard to stop. He was probably in his forties, with a boyish face and ginger hair brushed down over his forehead to make a Beatle fringe of a type fashionable when he started his sentence in the 1960s. All prisoners wear regulation clothing but each one favours a certain combination which he thinks suits him best. For T.C. it was grey flannels and blue-and-white striped shirt. I never saw him in any other outfit.

T.C. worked in the gardens. Later on, when I knew him better, he brought me a flowering plant from his barrow.

'What kind is it?' I asked.

'A begonia.' He explained how to water it and how long it could be expected to stay in bloom. The amount of natural light coming through the window of my cell was not sufficient to nourish it, however, and I had to give it away before it died.

T.C. and I had something in common: we both came from Glasgow. We talked our way through that subject quickly. I never found out how long it was since he'd been in the city, but more than the last third of his life had been spent in English prisons.

We moved on to other topics. Both of us took an interest in sport. Whereas I liked to watch boxing and football and follow the events, developments and internal politics of these and other sports, T.C.'s interest was limited to statistics. He was engaged in compiling vast tables of results, winners, champions, goal averages, and so on. When I tried to introduce the talents of individual footballers or personalities on the cricket scene into the conversation, it met with no response. T.C. would show a polite but total lack of interest, and return the conversation to his usual arithmetical vein: the likelihood of another name being added to the small number of clubs to have won the Scottish League, for example, or what chance Tottenham Hotspur had of beating Liverpool at home for the first time in almost three-quarters of a century. He was too far removed from the actual activity of sport, in both distance and time, to view it as more than a constantly changing set of numbers.

His tables, when completed, he told me, would be so extensive and thorough that by the time he came out of prison he would possess something with which he was going to astonish the experts themselves. Boxing champions in all divisions, and their opponents, were listed, together with their respective past records; the players, managers, team colours and achievements of every football club in the United Kingdom were set down, plus the form of each of the four British national teams; jockeys, trainers and owners of every winner and runner-up in every major track event this century were researched and tabulated. All this information was typed on sheets of lined paper which he revised and added to during most evenings in the education block.

Another hobby was to type out the words of pop and folk songs; a folder contained scores of lyrics to old tunes: 'Men of Harlech', 'Raindrops Keep Falling on my Head', 'I'm Getting Married in the Morning', and others; some he copied out of books, others were put down from memory. He showed them to me and invited me to read them over.

T.C. revealed one other intellectual interest: maps.

He liked to study a map of the area where the prison he was held in was situated. Perceptually, sensually, unfamiliar with its surrounding land-scape, barred from its forests, mountain ranges, rivers, green belts, towns and villages, T.C., by poring over the map, could construct a metaphor of the real country, an invisible equivalent of the scale model which an architect makes of a building. Here he might find a river previously known by reputation only, which he could trace with a finger back to its source; there a wood or a hill with an intriguing title, or a village with a comical name; over there perhaps a Roman road or a battlefield suggestive of the region's history. With these aids, T.C. familiarized himself with a land-scape he would never see.

On being moved to Lewes from his last prison, however, a misfortune had befallen him. Packing at short notice and in a hurry (prisoners are sometimes told only minutes in advance of the impending move), T.C. gathered up all his maps to take with him, but accidentally left behind the one he now needed most – the map of Sussex.

Here he was, having travelled at night in a van with small windows, not only without a mental picture of the town he was living in and its surrounding fields drawn from life, but lacking also the means to build up his own private plan of what it looked like.

Memory and his other mental hobbies apart, then, the walls of the prison were for him – in an overwhelmingly literal sense – the outer limits.

Postscript: This story has a curious sequel. I gave an account of T.C. and his maps to another experienced prisoner. He listened attentively and at the end I asked if he thought it was interesting. He thought for a moment before replying.

'Interesting, yes,' he said, 'but there are difficulties with it.'

When I asked what he meant he continued: 'Do you think they allow men in prison the means to help them plot their getaway?'

7 False Pretences

Opposite my room was a larger one, converted out of three cells, which served as the officers' tea-room. It was manned by a single prisoner who had the task of making tea and coffee and serving it to officers at tables, and also of taking the money – five pence a cup – for the service. The cash was banked in a tin box and handed over to the officer in charge of the tea-room at the end of the day.

The orderly was thus a 'trustie' (trustee), with a peculiar status, such as that of a junior staff member. As they involved a degree of independence, orderlies' jobs were much sought after, though there were many prisoners who would not consider working with prison officers.

The tea-room orderly's responsibility for cash gave him a sense of being trusted, which in turn permitted self-respect: you could tell by the self-conscious way in which he handled the little pieces of silver, always careful not to turn his back on his customers while dropping their money through the slot in the lid of the tin. The orderly also had an ear to officers' private conversations, which may explain why all four of the men who occupied the position during my time were 'sections', convicted prisoners awaiting sentence who were housed in C1, apart from the rest of C Wing, with whom they were forbidden contact.

I found it ironic but also rather appropriate that two of them were FP – the initials stand for false pretences – fraudsters, convicted on charges of deception. This was fitting because most FP merchants, in spite of their convictions, are highly conscious of the surfaces of respectability, which entails trustworthiness. FPs rarely mix, inside or out, with other criminals; they simply do not see themselves as criminal types. They usually adopt a certain standard of dress and behaviour, and regard their law-breaking as merely an unfortunate postscript to these standards, a necessary evil.

Richard was in most respects typical. I was entitled to use the tea-room, and once or twice a day – usually during lock-up periods when the tea-room was officially closed and no officers were present – I would sit in there and pass the time of day with him.

He was in his mid-thirties, of less than average height and neat appearance, with quoiffed reddish hair which, although it was his own, was so perfectly groomed that it might have been taken for a toupee. He made a point of impressing on me his need for personal cleanliness – it was a gross inconvenience for him to have to share a cell, as the sections had to do, often with someone whose ideas of hygiene did not match his own – and his good background, alluding frequently to the guest house his mother owned in Bournemouth, and to his habit of taking 'a full wash- down every evening, arms, body and legs, whether or not I've had a bath or shower during the day'.

Richard was intelligent and well-spoken; he had used his previous three- year sentence – also for fraud – to read the works of Goethe. One could imagine him on the outside as a salesman, the sort of person who likes to stay regularly in decent hotels and eat in restaurants, aspiring to own a superior type of car and making small but determined efforts at self- education, mainly but not exclusively for the purpose of improving his conversation, and therefore, in due course, his social standing.

He had to appear in Lewes Crown Court for sentencing four days before Christmas. The offences were not serious, the worst being a charge of having run up a hotel bill of over £400 which he tried to pay with a dud cheque. Others involved trying to leave restaurants without paying the bill and drawing money from banks with an unaccredited cheque book. The worst thing about them was that they were many. All placed the criminal in a socially enhancing situation – a hotel, a restaurant, a bank – and all were part of an effort to be touched with the shine of status. No outlaw is more conscious of social blessings than the FP merchant.

Richard expected to receive at least another three years for this list of offences, and in the tea-room the day before his court appearance he wondered aloud what he would do as a form of self-improvement this time.

'I like to set myself a course,' he said. 'Most of these blokes talk about nothing but crime – crimes they've committed and crimes they're going to commit, or say they are. Crime, crime, crime. I personally find it all terribly boring. I like to have a project which I can get involved in. It makes me feel that at least all this time isn't being wasted.'

On being asked my advice about which literary period he might study, I enquired if he had read many nineteenth-century novels. He hadn't, so I suggested the French: he could start with the works of Balzac, which were in the prison library, and it should be possible to lay hands on copies of novels by Zola and Flaubert. Richard thought this a fine idea. It gave him a little bit of encouragement for the next day, he said, when he would be standing before the judge. He was very nervous and expected small mercy from the judge. The charges weren't as serious as before, but the fact that he was back in the dock would by itself affect the judge's mood.

'In some ways I'll welcome the chance to do some reading,' he said. But I knew that he was only trying to comfort himself at the start of a long night ahead. I wished him luck.

'No doubt you'll see me back here tomorrow,' he said. 'At least Mr Saunders has said I can keep this job.'

There was comfort too in the thought of continuity. Richard would be likely to be sent back to Lewes after sentencing. For the long-term prisoner who is shipped straight from court to a large, strange dispersal prison, the prospect is more intimidating.

Next morning I went into a bookshop and purchased a copy of *Madame Bovary*, a consolatory Christmas present for the tea-maker. Then I turned the corner into Lewes High Street and walked up the steps to the court. Richard's name was on the noticeboard: Court 3.

I was slightly early, so I sat in the public gallery and watched two other cases before his, in both of which guilt had already been established. First was a woman accused of throwing a television from a fourth-storey window into the street. She was the mother of three children, now in care, and said that the loose wiring in the rented flat had so infuriated her that she lost control of herself and threw the set out of the window. She had been in custody before – both prison and mental hospital – and pleaded with the judge not to send her back to the latter, as he said he would, but to a prison. She had had 'enough of that Mental Health Act', she said. The judge listened stonily to her long plea, broken by sobs. He could see no reason to change his mind, and she was led away by two female prison officers.

Next was a burglar from Eastbourne. He was in his early twenties and had broken into a house while the family were watching television upstairs, stealing, among other things, a kitchen knife. He was arrested later the same evening, brandishing his booty outside a public house in the town. He too had a record, including two terms of imprisonment, but the judge commented that a third term would only conceal the problem and recommended instead a hostel place until social and psychological reports were prepared.

Finally –the last case before Christmas – Richard appeared in the dock with a prison officer on either side. When he looked round and saw me, the only person in the public gallery, I smiled and tried to show that I was there to lend support. But Richard's face registered surprise and then a hint of displeasure. He turned away quickly. I had the copy of *Madame Bovary* beside me on the bench in a paper bag: it was a very small gift; the real gift, I thought, was letting him know that there was someone with him.

Counsel had to remind his Honour of the charges. They were read out one by one, sordid details aired before everyone in the court. The accused had asked for twelve other offences 'to be taken into consideration'. Then, briefly, the details of his record was also laid bare. His previous arrest had involved over one hundred counts of deception and, before that, there had been burglary offences.

I began to understand why Richard wished me away. He had told me as we talked between ourselves in the tea-room about his case, but this was different, like being party to a public announcement of someone's private, dirty obsessions. He had never mentioned the burglaries, which he no doubt now regarded as a grubby and distasteful episode in his past, best forgotten. And there was something else. During our earliest conversations, Richard had talked about some larger crimes — I wasn't sure just where they fitted into his career — of being part of a team which had defrauded banks of £95,000, and, while a bankrupt with a criminal record, of opening an account and buying and furnishing a flat on the south coast. 'As well be hung for a sheep as for a lamb,' he had said then. And: 'No one can blame us for trying.'

No mention was made of these achievements now, even while his previous convictions were being discussed. As a criminal, Richard was undeniably, pathetically, petty. I wished I hadn't come, after all.

The judge was in a festive mood. Against expectation, he did not send Richard straight back to the prison he had come from, but to the same hostel as the burglar, until mid-January, giving time for reports and assessments to be made. He would be given employment and would have to sleep there every night, but would have some time of his own and would be free to walk the streets and go into pubs and shops like everybody else. This was a Christmas present indeed!

Richard politely thanked his Honour and left the dock with the escorting prison officers who had stood beside him throughout the hearing. As he went he did not even glance up at the public gallery. The barristers engaged in a bit of good-humoured banter with the judge, who responded in kind and wished all and sundry a Merry Christmas.

I left the court and stood on the steps outside, hoping to encounter Richard on his way to the hostel. A police car was parked at the entrance, which I thought might be for him, but eventually a drunk was bundled into it and driven away. Richard was gone. He had probably caught a bus to the hostel, grabbing his little interlude of freedom, or maybe even a taxi.

8 Christmas Day And The Devil On Boxing Day

It snowed for the first time, and then it seemed to snow all the time. The town was white and pretty, and I took my time walking up the High Street to the prison, pausing where a twitten dipped down to a valley packed full of rooftops and gables trimmed with snow. Beyond them, where the white land rose again, a frosty haze was lifting from the Downs. It was Christmas morning. Not for the first time, it occurred to me with a shock that they never saw Lewes like this, or any other way, except perhaps on visits to court, indeed that some had never known a proper experience of the countryside. Raised in town, sent to school and to work there until the first trouble, most would have set little time aside for weekends in the country.

Christmas Day was slightly different from other days. Only the men in the kitchen were working, plus a few cleaners; T.C. was out in the yard shovelling snow to clear a path from the gate to the door of the main block. He looked up when he saw me come through the gate.

'You must be mad coming in here today,' he said. 'It's different for us, we get paid for it.'

In the corridor outside my room, Gerald, the cleaner, went round and round with his broom and then his mop, whistling, 'Noel, Noel, the angels did sing', over and over. He had been at the carol service the previous evening.

There was bingo in the visiting room. I called out the numbers. Prizes were an ounce of tobacco or a pound to be spent in the canteen, with a jackpot of five pounds for three accumulated wins.

In the officers' tea-room there were raucous stories about the night before and miserable complaints about the morning after. One suggested a drop of prison hooch to cure a hangover, which raised a laugh, and then turned serious and spoke of the gallons of illicit brew which had been found in drains, plastic bags, bins, in use as false pillows, in the rafters, and other places.

'We find a drop, he puts his hands up and says it's a fair cop, then he gets on with making the next lot. It's a game; cops and robbers.'

In the kitchen the fifteen cooks were preparing to feed 500 men for the second time that day. There was turkey, roast potatoes, sprouts and carrots, preceded by soup and followed by Christmas pudding. Vegetarian, vegan, sugar-free and other diets are also catered for, and some meals are prepared in advance, which means that a variety of dishes are being made all at once. Pancakes are endlessly flipped and layered on greaseproof paper; meat and onions are mixed for tomorrow's stew; about fifty loaves are drawn from the oven and stacked on a multi-layered trolley beside another one with regiments of rock cakes. Five 'coppers' – pots large enough for cannibals to cook in – are lined up on one side of the kitchen's central area. In one, someone is stirring a massive dollop of mushy peas with a huge wooden spoon. Another copper is filled with water and, as it comes to the boil, tea bags the size of cushions are immersed in it: then the tea is ladled out into large plastic tea dispensers. Yet another copper is filled with porridge oats, for the next morning's breakfast. An officer comes along to inspect the mushy peas: 'That the gov'nor you got in there?'

At a small table in the officers' room a place is laid for the Governor to sit at when he comes to take his traditional daily sample of the food. He arrived, thanked the officers and men round about him for their service, then ate a few mouthfuls and pronounced it good. The prisoners nodded politely in response to his greeting as he left the kitchen.

'The King's taster', said one, 'has spoken.'

At a few minutes after 11 a.m., the trolleys were wheeled out to begin serving Christmas dinner.

Two weeks before Christmas a notice was pinned up in the wing:

> Please inform your visitors: 25, 26 December. There will be NO VISITS on these dates.

Visitors are dependants. For most, the dependency – family, financial – ceases when the man enters prison, and the tables are turned. Visitors bring into prison news of the world left behind – news in the sense less of hard information, which can be gleaned from newspapers, than of atmosphere and weather, family gossip, who's bought a new car, who's got a job; who's in trouble and who's out; a visitor really is a visitor from another world.

The Christmas ruling meant little to Paul, who got no visitors anyway. Christmas meant much to him, however, for he was one of the born again. He was another whose paranoia forbade him to talk to me.

A week earlier I had been talking to T.C. at the hot-plate, just before the tea-time trolleys arrived, when Paul appeared. Our eyes met at a distance of about thirty yards. Immediately he looked anxious. I had heard about a recent spin on his cell, after which, in a fit of explosive frustration, he had smashed his radio on the floor and hurled a television set over the landing whereupon it was caught on the safety wire, in place to catch jumpers as well as flying objects.

He had looked suspicious and defensive as he approached, and took up a position leaning against the radiator. He tried to smile but the smile drifted off and became a grimace. I greeted him with a nod and went on listening to T.C., as if our failure to meet did not concern me. But a few minutes later, when I was back inside my room, Paul put his head round the door and apologized for having accused me of being a spy. I thanked him and told him not to worry. Anyway, I could hardly protest the charge too strongly: I *was* a spy, although not in the sense he meant.

'I've got a lot of things on my mind right now,' he said.

'That's okay. I understand that.'

'I don't want no trouble, talking about it and all that. I've got too many things on my mind.'

'Of course, it wouldn't necessarily make them worse.'

'What wouldn't?'

'Talking about them. It might help to make them better.'

'Naw . . .' Paul waved his hand. 'I have to think about them one at a time. I know you were angry the last time, I could see it. I should never have walked through this door on that very first day.'

In one of our early conversations, we had talked about dreams. Paul told me that he had a recurring dream in which he died. It involved a fire in the house of someone he knew, someone in authority, usually a teacher or a social worker – and, knowing he was about to die, he always tried to wake up, without success. The dream terrified him and the thought of it returning sometimes stopped him sleeping.

I responded by saying that I also had dreams in which I was about to die, but that I always woke up before it happened.

'Ah,' Paul said quickly when I'd finished speaking, 'you see, that's the difference between you and me.'

Afterwards, when we happened to meet somewhere or pass each other on the landings, Paul would only greet me silently with his eyes, or offer a guarded hello. He was doing life for murder. He had been badly wounded by his guilt, and then further wounded by the prison's refusal to acknowledge that he carried his guilt with him everywhere; had it done so, then it would no longer have needed to punish him. (Or perhaps I had it

wrong: perhaps his continued and eternal punishment was his own choice
– the choice of the guilty man who falls to his knees and pleads for his
punishment, knowing that the craving created by his original crime can
never be satisfied.)

It was ironic, in view of his decision to have nothing to do with me, that
he was one of a very small number who asked me to do something illicit for
him. The first time it was only a bit of simple smuggling. I explained to him
that, were I found out, it could have disastrous consequences for me; and I
was in danger not only from screws, for it would be just as bad if the cons
got to think of me as a soft touch.

The next time, on Boxing Day, it was a more desperate request.

I met Paul on the landing of the fours as I was leaving someone's cell on
my way out of the prison.

'Here, Jim,' he said, 'want to come and have a look at some new things?'
The 'things' were ceramics, which Paul made at an evening arts and crafts
course, and made very well. He sounded more friendly than he had been
since our first meeting. He turned back towards his cell and I followed him
inside. There I was surprised to see another man, Pearce-Turnbull. I did not
like him. He called himself an Old Harrovian, dropped titles with the same
ease with which Paul cursed, and had a tiresome habit of beginning
sentences with 'When I was at Cambridge studying law. . .'. Pearce-
Turnbull had earlier been in the cell I had just left – I had flinched at his
reference to Paul as 'my boyfriend' – but had departed before me, saying
that he was going to take his bubble bath, 'alone, alas'.

Now I realized that my encounter with Paul was not accidental; he had
been put up to it by Pearce-Turnbull. For when we were inside the cell, Paul
closed the door and said:

'Here, you couldn't do us a favour, could you, Jim?'

'Probably not,' I said.

I felt his embarrassment immediately and was sorry for having spoken so
sharply. When I had refused his earlier suggestion to bring in something
from outside, he had reacted in the same way, immediately trying to
compensate with small talk and over-politeness.

For about a minute the three of us pretended to be having a conversation, waiting for the cue which would allow me to leave and relieve us
all. I was a little peeved at having been lured here under false pretences. No
doubt Paul would also be glad when I was gone. Pearce-Turnbull, however,
was more brazen. He raised the subject again. Then Paul, to cut the
atmosphere, explained in his fragmented manner what the problem was.

He had lately had an official Prison Visitor come to see him, a Mrs Reed. They are usually connected with the Church and come in on Friday evenings under the Chaplain's auspices. For the past month, however, she had been prevented from visiting; furthermore, although her mail was reaching him, he could tell by what it contained that his was not getting through to her. The visiting rights had apparently been withdrawn at a meeting between Mrs Reed and the Governor, at which the Chaplain was also present, and what Paul wished me to do was telephone Mrs Reed, and ask her to contact Pearce-Turnbull's aunt and tell her what had been said at the meeting. The aunt could then tell Pearce-Turnbull at her next visit, and he could pass it on to Paul.

That was all. He was clearly desperate to have the information.

'It's terrible, mate, it's not right. This Mrs Reed, she's done all kinds of things for me. She's my only fucking visitor.'

'Then why have they stopped her coming in?'

'It's *me*. You don't understand, Jim – these bastards are after my fucking head. They've got no right to tamper with my mail. They're not content with keeping me in this fucking horrible place for eight years, they want to get inside my head and start breaking it up. That's what they do, mate.'

I still wasn't really interested in doing illicit favours for prisoners which could interfere with my own privileges.

'I don't do this kind of thing, Paul,' I said. 'I never have. You know that.'

'That's all right, mate. That's cool,' he said nervously. He wanted to drop it. Pearce-Turnbull brought it up again.

'All we would like you to do . . .' he began, and continued in his mock-upper-class voice. The skin sagged below his mouth; half-moon spectacles attempted to give mean little eyes an intellectual appearance. I didn't trust him an inch. I knew that if I did something which wasn't allowed, no matter how trivial, he was just the sort to go chucking it around so that eventually it would rebound on me.

Still, Paul's anguish was hard to ignore. My desire to protect my own right of way within the prison suddenly seemed itself to be repressive, as if I had a vested interest in preventing him from alleviating his misery. Having welcomed the prisoners' instinct to expose their shadowed sides, what obligation had I to lighten the darkness when given a chance? To point to the rulebook and shrug one's shoulders seemed lame in the face of such profound torment. There was no question of breaching the code by approaching the authorities and speaking up for Paul. I wasn't sure that I understood all the details of the affair – I hadn't listened closely enough to take in all that he had told me, being preoccupied with my own side – but all I needed to know was written on Paul's face. The affair was cutting him deeply and fuelling his paranoia.

I wanted out. It was Boxing Day and I was expected at home for dinner and then at a party, and I was already late. There were one or two others on the fours I intended to look in on, people who could be relied upon not to trouble me with problems like this.

'Let me have this woman's phone number,' I said, standing up. I produced a notebook and wrote it down as he told me. 'I'm not promising anything, understand, but I'll see.'

'Thanks, Jim.'

'Don't thank me,' I replied, 'I haven't said I'll do anything.'

Next day I dialled the number. A pleasant, less than middle-aged voice answered and confirmed that she was Mrs Reed. I said I was calling on behalf of a prisoner at Lewes Prison and that I was just going to give her a message which he'd asked me to deliver, if she was willing to receive it, and then leave the matter in her hands. Yes, she said, she would take the message. I told her that Paul would like her to phone Pearce-Turnbull's aunt (whom she knew) and say what had happened at her meeting with the Governor, and so on. Mrs Reed readily agreed to do this. She seemed to believe with Paul and Pearce-Turnbull that it was terribly important, whatever it was about, and that it was cruelly unjust. She had the tone of someone embroiled in a plot. She said she would be praying for Paul, which was fine by me. She asked if I was a prison officer, or a Prison Visitor, or a teacher, or an ex-prisoner, or a minister. I said I was none of these.

'You don't wish to tell me who you are?'

'That's right.'

'Fine. I understand. Just tell Paul when you see him next that I'll be praying for him.'

I said I might.

Then I asked her a question: Why was she being obstructed in her wish to visit Paul?

'It's the work of a certain agency within the prison,' she said.

'The Governor?'

'No, not the Governor.'

'A prison officer?'

'No. It's the Chaplain actually.'

I was surprised. Before I said anything in reply, she continued:

'That man does not realize how he is being manipulated.'

'Manipulated by whom?'

There was no pause before she said: 'By the Devil. He's a decent man and he tries to do his job as well as he can, and the way he thinks it ought to be done, but he just cannot see how the Devil is working within him. . . .'

I put the receiver down. I regretted now that I had got involved with Mrs Reed and Pearce-Turnbull and poor, confused, tormented Paul. I couldn't yet know what consequences my action might have, perhaps none, but I knew it would have been better left without my intrusion, probably to die down and disappear. It still would, no doubt, but perhaps later rather than sooner.

That evening, I related the story to a friend.

'Anyway,' I said, 'Paul probably knows more about the Devil than she ever will.'

'Oh yes,' he replied, 'he *lives* with the Devil.'

9 At The Edge Of The Alphabet

The ventriloquist

Kenny killed his wife in a frenzied stabbing attack. He used a variety of knives from the kitchen drawer while their two children hid upstairs and his mother stood behind him, covered her face with her hands and screamed at him to stop.

Convicted on a charge of manslaughter, he was given a three-year sentence.

He hated and feared prison, longed to see his children and complained incessantly. He should have been afraid for the danger he was in from longer-serving cons because of his interminable moaning about his sentence, but appeared not even to be aware of their irritation.

At first, Kenny hung around my door without saying anything; just looking. He was tubby and boyish-faced, always wearing the prison sky-blue T-shirt. If my eyes met his, he would nod a greeting and maybe smile faintly. Eventually, I made a remark of a simple sort, he opened his mouth to start talking, and in a way never stopped.

He did not tell me everything at once, and he could never bring himself to talk openly about it, or even use simple, descriptive words to name events or objects. When he spoke of the killing he always referred to it as 'the incident': 'before the incident took place' . . . 'after the incident had occurred' . . . and, most awesomely, 'the incident which occurred between me and my wife'.

His wife's female friend, who had played a part in their separation was 'the third party'. He even avoided using the specific word for his beloved victim — her name, Mary — and referred to her as 'my wife' or 'my common-law wife, actually'. He spoke wistfully about her, using sentimental phrases and a nostalgic tone: 'We had a beautiful loving . . .'; he would pause to grope for the proper word, then let the sentence drop, as if something had just reminded him that she was dead and he had killed her.

Another way he had of describing things was to refer to pop songs, particularly Pink Floyd and the Beatles. 'Remember that line?' he'd say and then quote something, usually his favourite Pink Floyd hit from the 1970s:

> It riles them to believe
> That you perceive
> The webs they weave.

Kenny's speech was lavishly decorated with words like 'truth' and 'purity' and 'reality', with constant appeals to 'our fundamental natures' and references to 'more primitive people', always with the qualification that he was 'not being condescending, you understand, if anything I respect them more for it'.

He seemed to feel trapped by the network which had spread and snared him after the lethal deed. Kenny's preference for 'our fundamental natures' made me think he was bewildered to have discovered that acts gave rise to responsibilities.

On that first evening when he spoke to me he launched, without preliminary discussion, into an attack on 'the system', which, he said, did virtually nothing for prisoners after they left prison. He was not talking about finding them jobs, but about welfare and psychological help. Nobody did anything for you, he said. The welfare officer in this jail was an idiot. The doctors were idiots. The psychiatrists were complete idiots. None of them had the slightest understanding of how the human brain worked – 'a highly complex mechanism, am I right?'—nor, as far as he could see, had they any wish to understand. 'All they are interested in is their little power games and their pay packets.' He had received no help from them whatever. So, if a man committed another crime after his release and came back into prison, who could blame him?

'Who has the right to be surprised?' he asked.

'Maybe he has,' I said.

Kenny didn't hear. He only put his own question another way:

'Who is to blame, my friend – the man or the system?'

He was in no doubt about the answer, and clearly would not be led into reason or argument, even if only for the sake of testing his conclusion. The system was entirely at fault, period. And part of its fault was the way in which it divorced a man from his native surroundings by bringing him into prison, separating him from his natural habitat, from those who were nearest and dearest to him: 'Where he would get love and perhaps a return to life.'

'There's the world,' he said in the wistful tone he sometimes adopted, 'and there's this place, like a separate, spinning satellite.' And: 'You can never see yourself, only a reflection of yourself.'

Kenny felt he had a particular reason for being bitter at the aspect of the system which demanded separation: his children were in care.

'Beautiful kids, the most beautiful kids in the world, love their dad, poor kids, come up to see me in here — how would you like it, Jim?—the oldest one comes running up into my arms straight away. Does that sound like a kid who's scared of its father?'

The children were soon to be adopted. When that happened, Kenny would be unlikely to see them again. The prospect was one he found unbearable. He had lost his wife and now they were trying to take away his children as well.

'Hasn't a man got a right to care for his family, my friend, to love his kids and to treat them with loving kindness? Answer me — has he or has he not?'

He was in the process of contesting the order, but was finding it a difficult battle to fight from prison, especially since his solicitor, the welfare officer and the prison Chaplain were of the opposite opinion to him — namely, that adoption into a settled family was by far the best course for all.

After the first encounter I did what I could to avoid Kenny, mainly for fear of boredom. So preoccupied was he with his own talk, which he used to create a private world, that he was incapable of seeing or hearing anyone else. He used speech not to communicate meaning but to exclude it. It was the shield which enabled him to withstand the pain of memory and conscience. In any case, after two or three minutes I simply lost track of what he was saying. Having discovered what he believed to be a sympathetic ear, however, he was determined to track me down. He waited impatiently outside my door when I was busy with someone else, and hung around as before after unlocking times at one o'clock and six o'clock; only now, rather than eye me suspiciously, he was eager to tell me yet again about the family struggle — nothing new, just the same facts as before: the incident, the kids, the adoptive parents — 'nice people, I'm the first to admit'—the third party (not so nice), the doctor who was an idiot and the welfare officer who would do nothing at all to help. Nowadays he didn't even try to convince Kenny that what was bound to happen — the adoption — was in any case the best thing.

'And isn't that what they're here for, my friend, to help the inmates? If not for that, then what?'

He was even present when I attended a discussion group organized by the Chaplain, and bullied his way into the centre stage, silencing the guest speaker, telling us all once again about his woes with a system which, to his surprise – a surprise which was itself traumatic – increased his pain rather than relieved it.

I began to see Kenny's precious vocabulary (he never used prison slang), and the voice which was a runaway vehicle for it, as an effect of what he had done and the fear it had put into him. The words he had cultivated in order to hide his pain belonged to a world counter to that one in which the children, the knife, Mary and Mary's companion belonged. The words which adorned his speech were spells uttered to try to unlock him from bars and gates and cold walls, to gain the light of a clearer world, as others use sex or money or alcohol.

The voice is often used to mask the character of the speaker rather than to express it. People cultivate accents, adopt stammers, steal the voice of a hero, feign excitement or restraint, in disguises maintained, sometimes, throughout entire lifetimes. Kenny had trained his voice to take over from anxiety and guilt – both of which seemed to be constantly in pursuit of him. His voice was a din superimposed upon everything going on inside, and he himself was reduced to a cacophony of noises.

Son-of-the-chief

The following sentence was scrawled on the front of a prisoner's illicit journal:

> Speak of love not in their *own* voice but anothers.

No attribution was offered, nor a firm indication, such as quotation marks, that the sentence was originally someone else's and not his own.

If he did write it, it was difficult to see what he meant. The mixture of singular and plural; the emphasis; the third-person 'their'; the illiteracy of 'anothers'; the imperative mood (if it was so) . . . all obscured from the reader the meaning which had resonated so loudly within him that he been moved to preface his private writings with it.

This prisoner was a highly intelligent man. The journal, which he offered to let me read, was so vividly written that with a little work it would, I felt, have been publishable. Wary of stirring false hopes, I nevertheless told him so; he replied that it was the first time anything he had done had been praised.

He was homosexual and steeply inclined to romance, for which he found much scope in prison, although his homosexual desires were also a source of awful guilt. The journal entries were mainly about that, about his 'projections' while high on drugs, and about his religion, which frequently collided with his amorous and intoxicated lives.

An article which he wrote on the Creation began with this paragraph:

> In the beginning the Father allowed himself to be killed. In the magnitude of that act of love, the whole of Creation comes into its existence as a witness to the suffering in that death. The Father's purpose is that we, who are the effect of His death, may be raised to life in His resurrection. This was the 'Light' that came into the world.

I found this prose original and poetic, the sentences modulated by an ear closely attuned the cadences inherent in language. The main strength of his personal writing in his journal, however, for which he employed a different register, was its unsparing honesty, and, as a consequence of that, its self-accusatoriness. Even when the sentences expressed hurt – and he had experienced much hurt – they were redeemed from maudlin self-pity by an insistent confrontation with himself: 'My heart is filled with a pain that seems a thousand years old, a pain that asks is there no one person in the world I can really love and trust and I know the answer is NO.'

Yet the thrust of that honesty, which he employed like a weapon, was directed against his own continuing deceptive performance. It was a record of how he went on acting and speaking falsely to other prisoners, 'garnishing', as he put it, the story of his spell in the Foreign Legion while on the run from the Metropolitan Police, or dramatizing the reasons behind his return by claiming to have found the courage to come back and give himself up after a 'conversion in the desert'. The journal analysed these lies and castigated the liar. Next day, however, there would be a similar story. He housed in himself, then, welded together in one skin, both the boy who lies and the adult who advises him that telling the truth is better, both the coward and the hero, the frog and the prince. His perpetual, ruthless examination of his own conscience he must have believed to be redemptive – the act which might change the frog back into the prince.

This curious mixture extended to his physical being as well. He was a walking conundrum. His voice was well-spoken, its accent refined almost to the point of affectation, and his vocabulary rich and well-placed. The features of his face were those of an aristocratic Englishman, chiselled and handsome – with a trick of appearing strangely ugly at certain moments –

and his skin was black. His hair was cropped close to his skull to avoid the appearance of a negroid hairstyle, and he looked most of the time like an upper-class English sportsman constantly superimposed by his own shadow.

He was born in Manchester in 1949 after a liaison between a Nigerian medical student and a local woman who was already married with two children. Deciding that her latest, exotic production did not fit comfortably into this menage, she gave him away to Dr Barnardo's Homes at the age of three months, and there he remained for the next fifteen years.

Three things marked him and set him apart from the other children in that throng of helplessness: he was black, he was strangely intelligent and he was a thief.

'I was thieving at the age of four,' he said. 'It was the one thing everyone said about me, that I was dishonest.'

It was, at any rate, an identity, though hardly one to fit him for the world. Detention centre followed Barnardo's, borstal came after that, and then he graduated to prison. He was a state-raised convict.

His journal spoke of how much at home he felt in these institutions, each so alike in essence – 'You learn to sniff the operations of a place the moment you step inside'—and of how they gave him contentment, the contentment of the family, albeit of a comparatively wretched sort. In prison he lived as in a commune, having his own private room but secure in the knowledge that others, friends and brothers and lovers, were next door or a little way along the corridor. It was for him, a contemplative, the equivalent of the brothel which William Faulkner once said was the perfect residence for a writer: parties every night and peace to work in the morning.

One reaction to a life conditioned by rejection was his thorough loathing of his own face and body, as if he regretted the very circumstances of his creation. Out of this came the guilt about his sexual nature, and his attempts to change it. The journal told how he had tried to impose on himself a self-developed 'naked therapy'. This involved spending a certain amount of time with his naked body in an effort to make it acceptable to his inner self. In fact, as I have said, he was very handsome, but each night he would spend an hour lying on the bed, or sitting reading, with nothing on. The journal also mentioned a recurring dream in which he broke into shops and stole beautiful clothes with which to cover up his body. (This was, unfortunately, also a recurrence in reality, resulting in various short prison terms.) The thief was a frog, the dreamer a prince.

If he could reach agreement between his two inhabitants, by coming to terms with his physical state, then that might be an opening to a better future – a complete takeover by the adult who every day had to chastise the dishonest child. And one way he thought he might achieve this was by being accepted by his natural parents.

A journal entry referred to the communication he sent to a man in Nigeria:

> I received a very short note from Chief A – virtually saying nothing doing. I felt humiliated more than anything. The question is was I way off target or did he simply refuse to acknowledge the claim I was making. Well I shall not bury the incident and my desire. I want to belong to a family. Not just any family but that one which is particularly mine.

Chief A – was the man his mother had said was his father. It was not surprising that he should have such lofty origins. He spoke as if he 'didn't really belong' to this world of crime and spilt passion, of pledging himself to the better part of society, of self-improvement through study. Whether or not this illegitimate, state-raised, recalcitrant thief was the son of a chief I, of course, do not know, and neither, really, does he (the information from his mother, which seemed firm at first, turned out to be rather less certain later), but it fitted well into the myth which guided his life, of the frog prince whose native grace would eventually lead him to a proper inheritance. In a dream he is beautifully clothed . . . in a past before memory he is head of a tribe. . . .

What had passed in reality so far had been very different. After experiencing virtually every sort of institution invented by man – from the orphanage to the prison – he had been 'adopted' by a family from Devon, the parents of a lover, who accepted him and shared the warmth of their hearth. He still referred to them as Mum and Dad. He had lived together with them as a family for over a year, working in town.

'But every night when I came home from work,' he said, 'I used to walk up the path to the front door, fearing – expecting – that they would open it before I got there and say: "We don't want you any more."'

His other prominent fear – of not being able to dress well enough to be accepted in the world he aspired to – had led to an eight-month sentence on a charge of shopbreaking while he was living with the family. To his surprise they did not reject him, but visited him in prison and welcomed him back when he was released.

For the next few months everything was fine and they were happy once more. Then the same thing happened again. This time, after being charged, he was released on bail next morning.

'When I walked in the front door, the first thing I saw was the relief on Mum's face. She hugged me – I'll never forget that – and I told her it had all been a mistake.'

In time, however, the summons to appear in court arrived. He hid it from the family and decided to flee – to Manchester, his first home (though it never really was a home) – breaking into the household's fifty-pence gas meter on the way out.

'That theft was the first that had ever made me feel really guilty, suicidally guilty.'

Eventually he was picked up by the police and given a prison sentencce. The family felt that it had to let go of him, though it still had not abandoned him completely. However, he was resigned to the knowledge that for the time being at least his only real family consisted of fellow cons and, in a curious but unignorable way, the presence of a few prison officers.

I liked this man a lot and looked forward to our meetings. He was one of a few prisoners I would have become close friends with had we met in other circumstances. The conflict between honesty and self-deception in his character was infuriating, and yet I could see that it was quite ordinary in the sense of being common in many lives, and extraordinary only because few people are capable of bringing their intellect to bear on their experience with such conciseness as he was. He seemed to be struggling, really struggling, for independence from all the intangible forces confining him (as he had served only two out of a twelve-year sentence for armed robbery, it would be some time before he was free of the tangible forces) while at the same time indulging himself in them. Stealing, like homosexual love, he regarded as a vice, a secret and forbidden pleasure, which he must relinquish before offering himself up to be saved. But it also actually *was* himself – his body and soul, his essence. Therefore, he experienced a deep terror at the thought of letting it go.

'Speak of love not in their *own* voice but anothers'. Was this too, then, the epigraph on his journal, an accusation against himself – as in 'I find you guilty of speaking of love not in your own voice but anothers'? For while he seemed to be boldly pursuing the freedom to use his own voice – what else was his painfully honest journal for? – he still lazily carried on with actions which put him into situations where he could escape into another's: in dishonest love, for example, or the altered consciousness brought about by drugs.

With him as with some others — though few, if any, had his articulateness — the true voice floated like an enigma behind every sentence spoken or written. Yet his deeds contradicted it, and made audible the untrue voice. And he was always aware of this. What the voice said about the deed of its owner he took to be more truly him — the voice of the prince — yet he could not deny that the frog went about his actions regardless of what spells were cast over him. In order to hear the truth of what he said — and in order to relinquish the liberty of embroidering time by stealing or seducing or smoking — he would have had to disregard himself. The freedom language promised was too terrifying a prospect.

10 Working

Eight a.m. In the rain the prisoners troop to work. Even on the short walk between the exit from the main block and the plastics workshop, the rain begins to fall more heavily, but nobody hurries.

The factory is part of a miniature industrial complex at the south end of the prison, comprising several small workshops. The others are for engineering, bricklaying and painting and decorating courses. The plastics is the only proper manufacturing industry in the prison. The workshop itself consists of one large space, with an office for the three civilian instructors sectioned off in glass. The centre of the shop is occupied by a long table which is surrounded by several machines. Along one wall there is a row of latrines and water closets, the latter fronted by the same small doors as in the wing, which leave the occupant's head and feet visible at all times. The windows of the workshop are barred and entrance is made through a floor-to-ceiling barred gate, reinforced by a sliding door.

The machines do all the work. They are massive, compound affairs, constantly hissing and grinding and chuntering. The workshop teems with the noise and smell of industry, but that is a meagre disguise for the lethargy it creates and contains.

Thirty-five prisoners take off their coats and resume their occupations from the day before. Some are on duty by the machines, while others are trimming plastic mugs or plates. Those seated round the table are engaged in trimming or else sorting finished products into boxes. In the far corner, beneath a large window which admits the light needed for their task, a few men begin wielding delicate sable brushes in the meticulous painting of tunics and belts on the bodies of toy plastic soldiers.

After pressing the buttons which set the machines in motion, the operators pick up a book or a magazine (the morning newspapers have not yet arrived). One or two have already begun their endless tea making ritual. Some hardly bother to keep up the pretence of working at all; they write letters or stow away in a corner somewhere, chatting, if in a group, or watching the rain.

Hard labour. The nineteenth-century prison's hard-labour machine was a hand crank, a built-in fixture of the cell; pressure was regulated by the pound, and the unfortunate convict was kept turning the handle, sometimes on increasing weight introduced by the officer turning a screw – hence his nickname – for the whole of the long working day. When it first opened, the prison put men to work at other ingenious forms of unproductive labour. The treadwheel was one of these: convicts in separate cubicles stepped on to the ever-moving wheel and, as each stair dropped away from under their feet, continually had to step on to the next one. Although the wheel could be employed to pump water, it was more often used to 'grind the wind'.

Another form of hard labour was popular with the nineteenth-century authorities at Lewes: shot drill. This pre-machine-age industry consisted of lifting thirty-two-pound lead weights from here to there and back again. Sometimes the balls had to be stacked into pyramids at one end of a line, then carried back to be made into identical shapes at the other end. So it went on.

The treadwheels, shot drills and hand cranks have gone (in some places you can still see their remnants on the cell walls) and the plastics factory has replaced them.

The machine has a spiritless life and will of its own. It is the machine which has stirred the place into industry, giving the appearance of manufacture, creating the sour smell of hot plastic. . . . The man does not even have the contact with the machine which his predecessor had with the hated hand crank. All he is required to do is press the button which puts the machine into operation, and after that occasionally refill a funnel with polypropylene, adding now and then a pinch (one per cent) of colour – yellow, red or blue.

Today the colour is yellow. There is no reason why it should be, but it makes a change from yesterday, when it was blue. He tosses in the tiny coloured cubes. The machine grinds them into the melting polypropylene, digests the lot, then spits the wad into a mould, which punches it into the shape of a mug or a plate or an ashtray, which drops into the box at the operator's feet.

No doubt his place in the scheme could be automated too, if necessary, but that would cancel out the reasons for the mill's existence. The workshop exists only to provide him with employment – it is not profit-making – which is the Department's obligation. It is devised in perfect keeping with the system's view of its charges, as bodies.

Satisfied that the machine is running smoothly and will continue to do so for the next fifteen minutes or so, the operator lifts his book from its position face down on the floor at his feet and starts to read again: *In the Belly of the Beast* by Jack Henry Abbott, selections from a correspondence between the author and Norman Mailer. A few weeks before its publication in 1981, Abbott was released from prison; on the eve of the appearance of a notice in the *New York Times Book Review* which described him as 'a literary giant', he stabbed to death a young waiter outside a New York restaurant, for which he later received a further fifteen years. This paperback, now tattered from being passed around, came into the prison by an outside route, and the machine operator is not keen to be seen reading it. He shields the cover, with its loud colour and brash title, with his hand. Not that it is banned, strictly speaking, but it is not the sort of book the authorities would be likely to make available on the library shelves, and the promise of liberalism – held out so ostentatiously – can be broken at a second's notice. The rules, for example, say six books; today that rule is overlooked; if a reason should arise, it will be enforced tomorrow. So, when the escorting officer comes into the workshop at the end of the morning to check the shadow board, upon which tools are fitted to white shapes against a black background, and to rub the workers down before leading them back to C Wing for dinner, he keeps the title of his book out of sight.

He reads. The ferocity of Abbott's response inspires him; it also makes him ashamed to be sitting in lethargic attendance on this machine, to be another cog. He consoles himself that at least he is reading, looking up at the others. But he wishes that the machine would provoke a violent storm in him which would force him to destruction. Instead, he realizes that it is the peculiar nature of its violence which is slowly destroying him: its anonymity.

> I still stutter sometimes when I have to address a guard – address him without breaking the rules. I can cuss one out very eloquently or insult him, but that's when I've broken a rule or don't care if I do break one. It is strange to contemplate: people with a stuttering defect in society can usually *sing* without stuttering; well, I can *cuss* without stuttering. . . .

In the abstract he envies Abbot his extremity, his intensity, his evil, his suffering, for it has meant that he has remained unbroken. 'Beating the system' is a dream which all prisoners have; few succeed. The system is death and to beat it requires first that the convict risk his life against it in the way of a hero on the battlefield. If he overcomes, he will be changed and there will be no further need for 'rehabilitation' talk, for he will have accomplished his own transformation. The system resists this change with all its might.

To the left of his machine, a man is pruning electric switch covers from the small brown plastic stems on which they have budded. From each branch extend four covers and each has two open-ended outlets into which the pins of the plug will be fitted. On one of these four covers, on every branch, due to a malfunction of the machine, one outlet is partly obscured by a wart of plastic. Normally, the foreman would halt the machine and rectify this, but as things are he is content to have a man take a knife from the shadow board and cut it out, thereby creating another job.

It appears to have stopped raining outside. This is good news for him, because today, Friday, between one and two o'clock, there is practice for the football team, of which he is a member. The rain would mean the workout would be cancelled, and the deprivation would be punishing. His hour of football practice, together with the actual match played on a Sunday against an outside team, have come to seem like weekly spells of liberation: a time when he can lose himself in play. He is not a particularly skilled footballer – he is what's known as 'a worker'. He works – plays – to keep his little clue to freedom.

Providing work for 45,000 people is not an easy task for the Prison Department. If it is suggested that they be usefully employed in the community, objections are inevitably raised on grounds of security, prisoners' rights and, most pertinently, the high level of general unemployment. Efforts are made by the prison industries (they include uniform-making, broom-making, laundry, the making of window frames, printing police notebooks, as well as plastics) to obtain outside contract work, occasionally with success, but the industries are in some disarray since a group of officials of Prindus, the corporate identity of prison industries and farms, were remanded on charges of corruption in the early 1980s. At least Lewes can offer employment of some sort to all of its convicted men. In other prisons, workshops have been closed down because of alleged staff shortages; or there are not enough places; or there are simply no workshops. In July 1985 the Home Office announced a plan to close down a quarter of the 312 prison workshops. In prisons where there is a shortage of work, unemployed prisoners are kept locked in their cells, sometimes for twenty-three hours a day, often with one or two other men (known as two'd and three'd up).

At Lewes the plastics is the least attractive proposition for a worker. 'The cleaners' attracts the lazybones; it involves little work and a lot of hanging round idly on the wing. There is also 'the works', which has responsibility for maintenance of the prison, and 'the gardens', a relatively pleasant job which involves working outside the gate and is therefore open only to Category C prisoners. The luckiest, or cutest, find orderlies' jobs, which means acting as secretary in the Education Department or the library, as tea-maker and odd-job man in Reception, or as a waiter in the officers' mess or the tea-room on the wing. The average wage is about £2 per week. For most men this goes on tobacco. In addition, there are the three Vocational Training Courses, which actually come under the administration of the Education Department. For those who pass their tests, the reward is a City and Guilds Certificate. The apprenticeship is brief, and the level of skill attained is correspondingly modest. The engineering course, for example, lasts for twenty to twenty-four weeks. It is usually under-subscribed, and the instructors admit that it offers little real prospect of employment.

The only place in the prison where men are engaged in necessary work all the time is the kitchen. Long hours (6 a.m. till 6 p.m., six days a week) bring the reward of a wage more than twice as high as any other worker's, perks such as fresh milk, and the kitchen-worker's mark of distinction: a white T-shirt with a red K branded on the chest.

> I've wanted to convey to you what it means to be in prison after a childhood spent in penal institutions. To be in prison so long, it's difficult to remember exactly what you did to get there. So long, your fantasies of the free world are no longer easily distinguishable from what you 'know' the free world is really like. So long, that being free is exactly identical to a free man's dreams of heaven. To die and go to the free world. . . .

He can no longer concentrate on the book he has been reading and half-reading since just after eight. It induces a strange mixture of intense admiration and distraction. *To die and go to the free world.* . . . What can Abbott mean? What time is it? Somewhere near the middle of the morning (he purposely refrains from asking anyone the exact time). Suddenly, without willing it, he experiences a moment of fearless honesty during which he concludes that the system has him beaten, while recognizing in that very owning up the indestructible man he really is.

As he looks up from the page another yellow mug drops into the box. The sun comes out and, with the instantaneousness of a projection on a screen, casts a slab of sunlight on the floor beside him, sliced into neat oblong portions. The prospects for the afternoon are improving. Another yellow mug. Soon it will be spring. Another yellow mug.

One more of the system's many heads: tedium.

11 The System

The system is manifest in discipline; its nature is schematic and precise: drill, routine, programme; counting numbers, checking bodies, keeping times, turning keys exactly on cue; 'the rules state . . .', 'the rules forbid . . .'. It is invisible, passive, cruel: the system itself has no mercy, although it is sufficiently expansive that acts of mercy may be committed in its name. Prisoners blame their fates on it, jailers transfer responsibility to it. Few admit to having faith in it; no one can even demonstrate that it exists – it is simply the Grand Design.

The foundations of the system are laid in the stones of the prison, in its *architecture*.

It is designed to isolate: first, to isolate convicts from the community which produced them, and second, to isolate them from each other. The original aim was to prevent moral contamination, and also to deter conspiracy (this, and not respect for privacy, was what caused the single cells to replace the dormitory). It is designed, also, to facilitate surveillance.

The design is semi-panoptic: several wings radiating from a central hub, with cells ranged along the landings on each of three or four tiers. An officer standing in the hub, literally the heart of the prison, has a clear view along the ground-floor corridors of every wing, enabling him to keep watch on about one hundred cells, north, south, east and west. His counterpart on each of the upper landings is able, from his posting at the point closest to the hub, to maintain inspection of every cell along the length of the wing.

This design was first applied in Britain in the building of the 'model' prison, Pentonville, opened in 1842. It permitted the Separate System to be put into operation. Although it is long discredited in its original and extreme form, the Separate System is the pedigree for the organization by which prisons are run today.

The system, based on total solitary confinement, was developed in the United States and was first put into practice at the Eastern Penitentiary in Philadelphia. In 1834 William Crawford, a Home Office delegate, visited the Philadelphia prison, designed by John Haviland, and on his return wrote a report for the Home Secretary recommending that it be adopted in the United Kingdom.

Crawford contrasted the Philadelphia system favourably with that of another prison he inspected, Auburn, where the alternative Silent System was in force (backed up at Auburn by severe administration of corporal punishment). Under the Silent System, prisoners were locked in cells alone at night but worked communally, in strict silence, in the daytime.

> In judging of the comparative merits of the two systems, it will be seen that the discipline of Auburn is of a physical, that of Philadelphia of a moral character. The whip inflicts immediate pain, but solitude inspires permanent terror. The former degrades while it humiliates; the latter subdues but it does not debase. At Auburn the convict is uniformly treated with harshness, at Philadelphia with civility; the one contributes to harden, the other to soften the affections. Auburn stimulates vindictive feelings; Philadelphia induces habitual submission.

Before Crawford's recommendations were implemented in the building of Pentonville, prisoners were dealt with in Houses of Correction, in the Hulks – decommissioned naval vessels moored on the south coast or in the Thames – by transportation or by execution, none of which could be relied upon to 'soften the affections' and make ready for salvation through religious instruction. As executions declined during the first half of the nineteenth century, coinciding with the rise of philosophies of humanitarianism, and as countries receiving transportees began to object to the numbers landing on the shores, penal methods became more systematized, ostensibly with the aim of reform.

By comparison with the new regimes being put into practice in the middle of the nineteenth century, the eighteenth and early nineteenth-century prison was loosely administered, with jailers often earning their wages through the exploitation of their charges: by farming them out as labourers to private contractors, by exacting fees in exchange for release (even if the courts had acquitted them), by using women prisoners' wards as brothels, or by selling alcohol to all members of the prison population.

Moreover, sections of the prison were sometimes run by prisoners. The use of prisoners as 'trusties' or 'red bands' is as old as prisons themselves, and continues in practice today, but in the context of the new progressivism of the nineteenth century, it was felt to be getting out of hand when, as a former Chaplain of Millbank Prison reported to the Home Secretary in 1835, 'the employment of prisoners [as wardsmen] enables them also to act as spies upon the officer's movements, so as effectually to prevent him from restraining or detecting misconduct or irregularity'. In this way, the Chaplain went on to complain, 'the prisoner is the superintendent of the officer rather than the officer of him'.

In the newly built Pentonville such opportunities for exploitation, whether by jailers of prisoners or by prisoners of their privileges, ceased as total, rigid, solitary confinement became the order of the day. Prisons in the machine age were required to function like machines.

Every cell was equipped with a wash basin and water closet; exercise was taken in a walled pen attached to the cell; work was performed in solitude, often at a hard-labour machine, by operating a hand crank, producing nothing; inspection was maintained through the judas hole in the door of the cell; food was passed through a trap door, so that the officer was spared contact with his charge. Even at church – the influential presence behind the application of 'reformative' systems – the possibility of personal encounters with others was carefully removed, as the service was delivered to a congregation boxed in separate stables which permitted the occupant to look straight ahead at the chaplain but made it impossible to see to left or right. If it was necessary for prisoners to be exercised in groups or to assemble in any other way, then linen masks – 'beaks' – were worn, so as to prevent recognition by others. It was supposed that this would stop experienced criminals recognizing one another and conspiring, and that it would prevent the still impressionable offender being coerced by others upon release.

The immediate purpose of the Separate System in Britain was to fit convicts not for a return to society but for life in the colonies. In practice the long periods of isolation and total silence often succeeded in unfitting them for everything else. A high incidence of suicide, mental unbalance and absence of will was recorded among those subjected to the treatment. Hepworth Dickinson's *The London Prisons* (1850) describes one batch as 'literally unable to take care of themselves on a voyage. A day or two after the dead weight of silence and isolation was taken off, a great number of them became half-idiotic, that is, light-headed, low-spirited, silly and a few (the worst) subject to sudden faintings.'

Charles Dickens visited the Eastern Penitentiary and wrote about it in his *American Notes* (1842). He held 'this slow and daily tampering with the mysteries of the brain to be immeasurably worse than any torture of the body'.

The view was anticipated by the Visiting Justices of Lewes House of Correction, who submitted their report on the 'comparative merits of the Silent and Separate Systems' to the Secretary of State in 1838, four years after Crawford's enthusiasm for the American model was publicized. They favoured the Silent System for pragmatic as well as humanitarian reasons;

total separation as they conceived it would entail extensive alterations to the jail in North Street, necessitating the recruitment of new prison officers. As far as moral purposes were concerned, this system would, they believed, be totally effective in preventing contamination, while also protecting the 'well disposed Prisoner after his discharge . . . against the jeers and solicitations of his prison associates'. They recommended the wearing of masks by prisoners while in company, 'so made as to completely disguise the features without causing any inconvenience to the wearer'.

Before long, however, the building programme which was to adapt prison architecture to the Separate System was underway. Ten model prisons were built by mid-century, and the New Prison Lewes followed soon afterwards.

Even by then the harshest aspects of the Separate System were discredited, with doubts expressed in high places about the morality, and efficacy, of total solitude. Not long after Lewes was built the Pentonville commissioners, worried about the unbalancing effects of the regime, abolished the linen masks, the solitary exercise yards, and the stables in chapel (although these did not disappear from prisons altogether).

Solitude remained, and remains, however, a prominent feature of prison discipline. Punishment blocks in modern prisons embody, and frequently elaborate on, all the original principles of the Separate System. And other remnants of the system are still in evidence: for example, the rule at Lewes which forbids adult prisoners to speak to or have any kind of contact with the young prisoners being held on remand in A Wing, or the rule in other, stricter prisons, such as Wandsworth, whereby prisoners are permitted no free association and must walk round the central hub in an anti-clockwise direction, making eye-contact all but impossible. The bureaucracy and secrecy, the uniformity and depersonalization that characterize the contemporary prison system, which prisoners revile with such bitter ferocity and which they are often held to be imagining, were founded and formed in the Separate System.

Examples abound locally of the cruel methods of anonymous surveillance, culminating in the file of reports kept on every prisoner – by governors, prison officers, probation officers, chaplain, doctor, teachers – which he is forbidden to see. Always conscious of the development of this file, and already in a position to trust no one, he can quite easily begin to believe that his puppeteers are deliberately manoeuvring him in the direction opposite to that in which his best interests lie. He can find no one to blame: prison officers and governors alike are merely technicians of a system which is invisible – and perfect, in the sense that it is unassailable.

Strict solitary confinement leaves no room for privacy, a condition defined in opposition to the possibility of community. The modifications to the system have altered that, since most prisoners are now permitted to associate with one another, but genuine privacy is still infeasible.

Among the cruellest results is the lack of privacy of the flesh. Urine and faeces are slopped out in procession each morning and, where necessary, after each of the lock-up periods following dinner and tea. In the lavatories the water closets are shielded by half-doors which leave parts of the body visible. Bathing, including showers and baths, must be performed in company.

Although the prisoner spends up to two-thirds of the day in his cell, he never has the privilege of locking and unlocking it himself. And an officer can come along at any time and open the door (when it happened in my presence, sometimes for my benefit, I felt ashamed) or else peep through the judas hole. Generations of prisoners have devised ways of contesting these intrusions by wedging up the door, or taping the judas eye, or by strategic placing of the person inside the cell so as to keep out of sight of the inquisitive outsider. Seeking privacy, he becomes a fugitive.

As recorded in the prison Chaplain's notebook, prisoners learn to communicate secretly. It is no longer necessary to go to the lengths of coughing, rapping, or placing fingers on the mouth or ears, but it is still necessary to have codes and secrets which are inscrutable. It may be something simple: an item of prison slang; a knowledge of where the hooch is stored; which among the prison officers is bringing illicit matter into the prison, and it may even be a lie, so compelling is the need to appear to possess a secret.

There is one, very ugly, way in which the system has reversed the power of secrecy so that it can be used against the prisoner. It is this:

The wing has a letter box attached to the wall near the wing office where prisoners post their outgoing mail. When the box is emptied the letters are taken upstairs to an office on the fours where the officers acting as prison censors read them, checking for defamation of prison officers, breaches of security, or just to ensure that they are handwritten. (The censor, of course, also has a hand in the prisoner's evolution of codes; some letters are written almost entirely in code, so discreetly that the censor never notices.)

Prisoners are allowed one free letter a week, second class, with the option of paying the extra postage to make it up to first class. In addition they are allowed three letters 'canteen', which means they buy the materials themselves. Prisoners may post letters to their friends in other prisons – a practice until recently forbidden – if they can discover where they are.

But the letter box has another, quite different, use. Every now and then the officer emptying the box finds an unsigned memo addressed to him, or to any prison officer.

'Dear Sir', it begins – or perhaps it dispenses with salutations – 'Greene on the twos will be having a party tonight. Puffers only invited.' Or else: 'Grey on four landing was using an unusual knife to cut his bread this morning.' Or just: 'Black's visitors bring him drugs.'

Of all the scapegoats, the grass is the most reviled. Condemned by the law and hated by his fellows, he is twice guilty, and therefore craves punishment twice as determinedly as anyone else.

12 The Voice (II): A Grass

Stuart's face was a graphic record of his inner wretchedness. He was bespectacled, prematurely bald with a permanent red sore on the pate, had a high forehead and a distemperately blotchy complexion. When he talked about something he felt strongly about – and he felt strongly about everything – one of his eyes half-closed, its lid flickering rapidly, while the other sometimes glared at whoever he was talking to, sometimes rolled back in his head. He had an intellectual face which together with his voice, could have belonged to a university don. He talked quickly and fluently, making fine distinctions and astute observations, and responding swiftly to argument.

His current sentence – life, for the murder of a homosexual lover – was not his first. Now in his mid-thirties, he had spent over half his life in places of confinement. He held obstinate, marxist-based views on the prison system and its relation to society at large. No matter where a conversation began, Stuart would lead it back to his idea that crime was a product of the capitalist system which sets people in competition with one another and measures value in economic terms. He was firmly of the view that prisons were breeding grounds of further crimes.

Stuart's conversation, although characterized by high intelligence, was dependent on jargon. When it wasn't clogged up by the words of marxism, it was by those peculiar to the study of psychiatry, which he was engaged in studying privately, holding himself to be mentally ill, the possessor, he said, of 'an over-wrought conscience'. When I mentioned his dependence on jargon he replied that he hadn't thought himself intelligent until he began reading in psychiatry. Since then his primary object of study had been himself. He was both doctor and patient, and had only begun to accept his own worth since establishing the process of explaining himself to himself.

No one, so far as I could see, liked him, staff or prisoners. Several times I instigated conversations with him only to end up being verbally attacked; at various points he charged me with being a 'dilettante', a 'wishy-washy liberal', and of wanting to write 'a cosy little book about Lewes Prison'. My presence inside, though he never gave me a chance to explain it, rankled with him and always seemed likely to add heat to the violence which simmered below the surface of his every action. I was surprised, therefore, when he stopped me in the corridor near the wing office one evening and asked if I still had my tape recorder. I said I did. He then asked if he could come and see me in the morning and read something into it, which he did. It was unexpectedly free of the jargon which muddied his conversation.

At the close, he stood up and said he felt better now that I had it on tape. 'You might want to do something with that,' he said, 'if in two or three months' time you hear that I've been killed or something.'

'I was sentenced to life imprisonment in March 1973 and, on being advised that I was to be sent to A—Prison, sent a petition to the Home Office warning of the dire danger of being placed in the same prison as Roger Tizard. I was principal witness for the prosecution against Mr Tizard, who was sentenced to life imprisonment and who, after his trial, vowed to kill me. The contents of my petition were not acted upon by the Home Office and in 1977 Tizard showed prisoners at A—the statement I had made to the police during the enquiry into his case.

I suffer from manic depression and am also bisexually orientated, possibly as a result of having been kept for too long in an all-male environment, with a greater bias towards homosexuality. At the time Tizard passed the statement round, a drug addict in A—was attempting to manipulate my homosexual feelings in endeavouring to secure finance for his proposed illicit drug smuggling into the prison. This latter man also managed to manipulate the homosexual feelings of another man in A—who, like me at the time, was voluntarily attending group therapy meetings run by a consultant psychiatrist. In this way, my entire psycho-social history came into the possession of the drugs fraternity at A—, who, at rotated drugs gatherings, divulged it to each other.

Prisoners cannot abide what is termed a "grass", and arising from their own feelings of guilt and from the effects of Tizard's mischief, a concerted vendetta of victimization was mounted against me by the prisoners who monitored all my behaviour and reported back among themselves.

The prison authorities, despite many requests, would not remove me from A—, notwithstanding that it was obvious I was being badly bullied and badly victimized. I didn't want to make my own situation worse by complaining, as any staff intervention would have been deduced as originating from me. It was known by staff that I knew of

the drug trafficking into the prison, and on more than one occasion it
was intimated that if I was prepared to divulge names and methods my
request for a transfer would be looked upon more favourably. I didn't
like my feelings being manipulated by drug abusers in prison and I
could see plainly with my own eyes that prison officers were too
cowardly to deal with the prison drug problem themselves, finding it
easier to turn a blind eye to it, the rationale being that it kept the
prisoners happy and out of the way, giving the prison officers a happy
and peaceful life. Yet all sorts of actions of violence and damage arise
from drug-taking, quite apart from the lucrative living made by the drug
barons, as prisoners find themselves helplessly in debt and have to use
their visitors or borrow from others in trying to cope. It cannot be right,
that by non-action the prison officers implicitly endorse the values
which found the attitudes which lead to people committing crimes in
the first place.

At any rate, I tried to carry on at A—as best I could, but I lived
through moments of very great fear, if not terror. At times I was
completely suffused with tense anxiety and too frightened to come out
of my cell. In January 1979 I requested an interview with the Governor
at A—, and in the presence of a prison officer told the whole sad, sordid
story, all of it, named names and methods of drug traffickers, and
protested that the prison officers already knew but were too cowardly
to take any action. This resulted in my being transferred as an
emergency case from A—to B—, in February 1979. But at the same time
another man, Watts, was similarly transferred and, via the Prison
Officers' Association, prisoners at B—were advised that I was what they
termed a "threat". The man Watts quickly set about advising prisoners
there that I am what criminals term in their vernacular a grass. He also
divulged my complete psycho-social history to other prisoners. A
Probation Office report submitted to the Home Office at the time, reads
in part: "He had a hard time at A—and came here suffering from the
effects of strain and stress."

I experienced all manner of difficulty at B—: my cell was set on fire;
my tea was urinated into; my carrier bag was defecated into; I was
homosexually snared, and my feelings of guilt and jealousy mercilessly
played upon by the vast core of drug takers there; I was set up by
prisoners and placed on report; a brick was thrown through the
window of my workplace; an illicitly brewed bucket of beer was placed
in my cell – I openly and in full view tossed the contents on to the floor

of the wing; I was assaulted; money sent in by friends mysteriously
failed to materialize and the Governor ordered a police enquiry. I was
incessantly intimidated and sexually tantalized such that my life came to
a stop.

Because I was under such fear, frustration and general pressure, it
was decided I should go to Grendon Psychiatric Prison. But because I
realized that prison officers there saw this as a soft option, I
immediately elected to leave and was returned to B——. The Governor
gave me a job which gave me sufficient freedom of movement to keep
away from other prisoners, but the fact of his doing that was unpopular
with prison officers as well as the prisoners themselves. Eventually, I
was provoked by two prison officers and had the job taken away, and
this resulted in intensified difficulties as prisoners were able to abuse me
in the workshop.

This continued until the end of 1982. I was transferred to C——Prison.
In May of that year, on being told I would be sent to C——, I wrote to an
MP complaining that I was certain the transfer would be very
dangerous, if not disastrous. The reason for this was that the man who
had set fire to my cell in B——, one Francis Gibson, was also in C——. This
was forwarded to Lord Elton, who advised that no trace of the fire
could be found and accordingly I would go to C——. In fact what had
happened was that the prison officers simply omitted to document a
record of the incident which, yet, was in the knowledge of the Governor
of B——Prison.

Exactly what I thought would happen at C——happened. My feelings
of homosexual guilt and jealousy were played upon, resulting from the
considerable rumours spread by Gibson, and arising from
fear-responses born to pressure of these rumours, I suffered an
unusually large and oppressive number of disciplinary measures,
culminating in my having to be taken to an outside hospital for
emergency treatment involving some thirty stitches after I'd been
viciously attacked in the prison gym.

A prisoner was duly convicted of that attack before the Board of
Visitors, and the Governor was compelled, through fears for my safety,
to hold me in isolation. As a protest against my original advice and
suggestions being negligently disregarded, I staged a hunger strike, and
was removed to Lewes Prison at the beginning of 1984 – yet again to be
housed with Gibson.

I wrote again to my MP and complained: 1) of the presence of Gibson in Lewes; 2) of victimization; 3) of negligence; 4) of the unlikelihood of my parole representation being just; and 5) of the possibility of further violent attack.

Unfortunately for me, there is a basic flaw in my condition of mind which has been unremittingly exploited by the drugs fraternity in prison. I am afraid of love being withdrawn. As a result of a series of attachments and losses, I've become hate-full and psychically withdrawn. This has been caused by the drugs fraternity in prison, so that I walk around so to speak blind and naked.

I have been living in fear at Lewes because the place is infested with drugs. After a number of incidents and events I finally decided to complain to the police in Lewes about the level of drug-taking in the prison.

I am also particularly vulnerable to rejection and this too has been exploited. I can't continue bottling this up all the time, all the hurt and pain. I've been made to suffer and one day it's bound to come out. It's only guilt which keeps it in. It is impossible for me to form any proper social relationships in prison because people's minds have been turned against me as a result of infection by prison drug-abusers and because of the greed and dishonesty of drug barons. If I talk with staff I'm supposed to be ingratiating myself, while on the inmates' side I'm disowned as a grassing, raving poof. I simply cannot win. Everything I do is wrong. I feel exposed and threatened in all my actions.'

13 The Uniform

At four-thirty, one Friday evening, I came out of my room to find the usual group congregating in the corridor in expectation of the tea trolleys. It was the usual group, but it had a different atmosphere. A nervous buzz emanated from the swarm. Something was in the air.

I moved over to join Billy Miles, a Dennis-the-menace figure who was always well-tuned to the prison grapevine, and therefore useful in providing morsels of information or gossip.

Rumour had it – or perhaps only he had it – that there was going to be a ghosting. Bulletproof Joe, a big Welsh con doing life – so-called because of the amount of lead he carried around inside him – feared it was going to be him, and had gone down to the wing office to demand an explanation. Ghostings were sorry affairs: they involved a sudden descent by several prison officers, designed to catch the body by surprise. He is parcelled up and despatched to another prison by moonlight, ignorant of his new home until after he is locked into one of its corners.

If it was to be Joe, they weren't likely to tell him in advance: a previous ghosting had required – so legend had it – twenty prison officers and the use of dogs, two of which Joe had killed while the flitting took place.

(Joe was a big-hearted man and a Christian. During a chaplaincy meeting once, he had sat all evening murmuring over his Bible, looking up only to announce that on the day of his release he was going to come back with a gun and two bullets which he had promised to a certain officer: 'One I'll put through his head: I'll say this is to help you keep an open mind. And with the other I'll lay him out: and this is to bring you back down to earth.' Everybody laughed.)

The prisoners working outside the gate had been brought in early and a notice on the wing blackboard stated that no Prison Visitors would be permitted to come in this evening, as they usually did on Fridays.

At six o'clock, after tea, the prisoners remained locked in their cells. The drama which ensued had nothing to do with Bulletproof Joe, or with a ghosting.

When the prison was fully silent, the sniffer dogs were led in by their handlers. There were four of them. They went to selected cells in C Wing (and subsequently throughout the prison), threw open the doors and searched them from top to bottom. Fortunately for some, warnings were shouted through the bars from one cell to another and from lower to upper landings; buckets of hooch were poured out of windows so rapidly it sounded like the briefest of cloudbursts; lumps of hash were bunged in the anus, hidden outside the window or swallowed, and folding money was similarly disposed of.

Next morning those placed on report for possession of drugs or anything else appeared at adjudication hearings in the block, where summary justice was dispensed.

No prisoner ever sees the officer without his uniform, just as the officer never has the opportunity of viewing the convict outside his prison grey. Since each uniform is determined to confer a status, then, everything which their relationship consists of emanates from the confrontation of these two sets of clothes.

This is not how the Governor would like it to be, but it is inevitably so. The man who was chatting to you about your wife and children at four o'clock is the same as the officer who is forcing you to submit to a search, or ghosting you out, at six. 'I was only doing my job,' he says, and so he was; but the convict's vision of him as a man is cancelled out by his actions as an officer.

The prison officer's uniform is not merely a set of clothes. He depends on it, falls back on it, uses it to establish authority when he senses that his personal capacity is failing – or perhaps he uses it to protect that capacity from ever having to be put to the test, fearful lest he should find it wanting, or even vacant.

The prisoner, on the other hand, has every excuse for not attributing human qualities to the man who locks him up, bosses and bullies him (sometimes without realizing it, which could make it worse) and generally refuses to recognize that he is more than just a body, an element of the vital routine. Both are thus trapped in a single cage, divided by a glass partition: seeing each other, mouthing messages, signalling but not communicating.

The aim of the regime at Lewes was to establish a more caring role for the prison officer, to deepen the bond between officer and convict – between us and them. The aim is admirable and was in some ways success-ful. There were no tales of beatings at Lewes, although prisoners brought with them stories from other prisons which one seldom had a reason to disbelieve. Prisoners and prison officers were often on first-name terms, something which astounded those arriving from the fiercer dispersal prisons. (Some took it, as they took everything, as just another tactic in the system's continual war against them, and wanted to return to the harsh prisons which at least they could trust. In this way what is conceived as the regime's kindest feature is received in some quarters as its cruellest.) One often heard of a prison officer bringing in a foreign newspaper for a homesick prisoner, or, say, a sample for dissection for a biology student.

But no matter how hard he tries, the prison officer can never step out of his uniform, and therefore away from his power – the power which creates the divide, which compels him to view the prisoner as his charge, the material he has to work with, an appendage to the key he carries, a body.

The question of how much goodwill was destroyed by the events of the Friday when they brought in the dogs, was one which exercised, and generally vexed, the minds behind the administration of the prison. The order to do so had come from above. In any case, the most likely answer is: very little; for there was little there to be destroyed in the first place. The prisoner always knows – cannot afford not to know – that the uniform is a licence to use force, whenever circumstances require it. The prisoner lives with the knowledge, which the officer often seems to wish to avoid, that when a conflict boils down to violence, everything under the sun will support the officer in his use of force, whereas the prisoner himself will be helpless. This knowledge is behind every encounter between prisoner and prison officer.

The officers frequently attempted to deflect that knowledge on the prisoners' side by making the accusation of lying. I was frequently told that 'all prisoners' were liars, that I should not believe a single word a prisoner uttered. The possibility of my believing 'everything the inmates tell you' was seen by the Prison Officers' Association as a major obstacle to admitting me into the prison. Once, while I was talking to a prisoner in the education department, the officer on duty came along and silently held up a sign in front of my eyes: 'I'ts [sic] all lies.'

Again and again, I was asked: Are you only going to be talking to prisoners? No, I'd say, prison officers as well.

'You'll get the truth, then.'

Since prisoners told me many uncomplimentary things about themselves (and some complimentary things about officers) this much-repeated advice was misdirected. I was not so naive as to think that no con would try to deceive me – in both large and small ways –or use me as a sounding board for the more ridiculous fantasies (or secrets) which prison life breeds, but I began to see that the myth of the unbelievable prisoner had its beginnings in the fears of prison officers – the fear, to be a little more precise, that behind their backs the truth was being told about them, that the people speaking could see beyond the uniform to the person wearing it.

The uniform itself is of a military cut and navy-blue in colour. A large percentage of the officers enter the service from the armed forces. The basic officer wears a policeman's blue shirt and a peaked cap; senior officers are distinguished by a white shirt and one pip on the lapel, while the principal officer has two pips; the chief officer has two pips and a crown and chief officer class 1 has two of each. After that come the governor grades who dress in civilian clothes; assistant governor, of which there are three at Lewes – one in charge of each of the three main wings – deputy governor and then the governor of the prison himself.

Besides the officers and governors, there are many other full-time staff, working in administration, in prison industries, in the gardens, in education. They do not dress in uniform and are called 'civvies', fortifying the military overtone which pervades the running of the prison.

Full-time civilian staff, like the officers, carry keys: the pass key is attached to a long, looping chain which the officer links to his trouser belt. When not in use the key stays in his pocket or else in a small holster worn at the hip. If the key is the officer's weapon, it is also his largesse, granting him the power to make even the most arrogant con lower his head and say, 'Will you let me through this gate, please.'

The use of ranks as titles is obligatory among staff in discussion of any matter pertaining to the prison; officers address their equals as 'Mr' and their superiors as 'Sir'. A high standard of efficiency and discipline all round is regarded, by the uniformed staff in particular (governors are often scorned, though not necessarily here, for their liberalism), as essential to a proper administration of the prison.

This leads to the most elementary of the many contradictions which beset the man in his role as prison officer. For while his first task, in accordance with the Prison Department's official definition of the duty of the prison service, must be 'To keep in custody . . . sentenced prisoners for the duration of their sentence', another aspect of his role – and one which is made much of at Lewes – is to provide for the prisoner 'as full a life as is consistent with the facts of custody', though the latter consideration must necessarily be subordinated to the former: containment, that is, *then* reform.

The emphasis on the priority of containment, however, has meant that over the years, particularly of the first half of this century, the prison officer's part in the process of reformation of the prisoner has shrunk to an almost invisible size. Officially the modern prison officer has no professional obligation to attempt to establish a relationship with his charge – although he is frequently encouraged to do so – which involves more personal contact than is implicit in the business of locking and unlocking the doors to keep him in or let him out: in short, in controlling him.

Of course the place of reformative methods and practices has not disappeared since it ceased being solely the responsibility of the clergy; rather, it has been handed over to the social services. This is a comparatively recent innovation (since the 1950s) which has not, on the whole, been welcomed by prison officers. In a memorandum published by the Prison Officers' Association in 1963, 'The Role of the Prison Officer', the following plaintive description of a member's daily routine is found:

> A day's duty for an officer usually comprises nothing more or less than unlocking the men and locking them up again; escorting them to exercise, to the workshops and back again inside the prison; feeding them and, at the end of the day, finally locking them up and checking them in for the night.

This could serve as an accurate, if very basic, summary of the role of today's prison officer, though most officers do not approve of it and are hopeful of changing it. The POA professes to seek to take over the role of the welfare agencies within the prison. In so doing they argue that the prison officer is in a better position to understand and cope with the problems, major and minor, which arise in the day-to-day life of every prisoner, as he is in constant contact with him. The welfare officer is an outsider who sees the prisoner only in the artificial light of a man-to-man interview in the protected arena of the welfare officer's room. Moreover, the welfare officer is in the prison only during office hours, and those hours coincide with the time during which most prisoners are at work. The prison officer, on the other hand, maintains the POA, is on duty at all hours and, most importantly, is available during the association period in the evening, between six and eight-thirty. At these times, prison officers have the opportunity to engage prisoners in conversations leading to discussion of a particular problem or grievance, which may be solved without the involvement of any other party, to the mutual peace of mind. The result, it is argued, is a deepening of the relationship. If this role is denied the prison officer, if his duties are restricted to those of a turnkey – one nuance of the word 'screw' — then the impersonality already implicit in the relationship is bound to increase, leading, eventually, to violence.

Michael Hull was in favour of the prison officer sharing the function of the welfare department. A sincere, earnest man who approached his tasks thoughtfully and was generally liked by cons, he made a good advert for the system. He had sought, and been granted, permission to talk about his occupation to local community groups, and had organized and participated in more than one local radio programme on life in prison, in which a number of prisoners were also involved.

He was the first prison officer I was introduced to, and was chosen by the Governor to be one of my two links with the system (the other was an assistant governor), a role he fulfilled discreetly, without ever interfering with my movements and actions.

One afternoon we had a long talk in my room, during which he set out his own conception of the prison officer's responsibilities.

'There are good officers, bad officers and in-between officers. The inmate soon gets to know which ones he can talk to and he finds that if he can get a straight answer then he will be prepared to have a conversation. I don't think the uniform stands in his way. In fact, there are many inmates who would far rather have an officer deal with their personal problems than they would a member of the welfare department. I think it's a lot to the credit of the officers that they do, because it means there's been a relationship built up between them. In many ways that relationship saves the prisons of this country from great disturbances. And if officers are being honest with themselves they know that it's a far better situation to be able to come to work and talk to inmates and have some form of relationship with them, than to come in and always have this very cold atmosphere where there's no dialogue and you don't know what's going on.'

The division of tasks within the prison — containment to this group, welfare to that — leads to one of the most persistent and unpleasant rumours about the prison officer, which pursues him no matter how he wriggles to escape it: the picture of him as, at best, nothing but a brisk disciplinarian constantly wielding his key, and, at worst, as a sadistic brute. The latter suggestion he regards as an ugly stain on his office and after talking to any group of prison officers one is left in no doubt that he would dearly like to have it removed.

Michael Hull's idealism was greater than most, and he was keen to emphasize how it was possible to regard the tasks of the prison officer vocationally.

'You learn right from training school. You spend first of all a month at a prison, to find out if you're going to be able to do the job at all – things such as if you're claustrophobic or not. It's surprising how many people don't realize they're claustrophobic until going into a prison brings it out in them. So before they spend thousands of pounds training you they're obviously going to let you get the feel of the type of environment in which you're going to be working.

'When you go to the training school you're taught everything about the job. Obviously you've got to know all the rules pertaining to the prisoner: what he's entitled to, and all that sort of thing. You've also got to know about self-defence: if you're dealing with violent inmates you have to feel confident of being able to defend yourself. You've got to know a bit about first-aid as well.

'But they put a lot of emphasis on understanding human behaviour, on communication between yourself and the inmates. They make you look at problems of alcoholics, gamblers, drug addicts – how their addiction affects them, how you can cope with them.

'I found training school one of the most enjoyable parts of my service, because I never realized how complex the job was until they started explaining what it involved. You're dealing with *people*, they say, everybody you're going to be dealing with is different, just the same as all the staff are different. You discover that you have to analyse yourself before you can analyse anybody else: one of the things about dealing with people for any length of time is that if you try to create a false front, invariably, sooner or later, you're going to let it slip and the inmate is going to see it. When he sees it, he immediately loses any trust he may have had in you.

'Now, that can be a problem for some officers. They may feel: Oh, I don't want to show this side of my character because it won't be seen very favourably by inmates; or: I've got a uniform on so now I've got to act as a very dominant person, look really in charge of myself, sergeant majorish-type. Now that I've got a uniform on, that's the way they expect me to be. I suppose it all comes down to having confidence and self-assurance, that you're able to be your normal self and cope with inmates at the same time.

'You're always going to have that barrier: you're the screws and we're the cons – and however much we may talk to you there's always going to be that barrier. But I think that if you spend any length of time with a person, there is a form of respect builds up between you: *he* needs you as much as you need him.

'So, the first thing you have to be is a good listener: he wants someone to talk to, he wants someone who is sensitive enough to listen and not to mock – he doesn't necessarily want advice, he just wants to get it off his chest. Relationships between inmates and their families – particularly between men and their wives – can be a very sensitive area. I think it's to *our* advantage as well as his own that he talks about it. I'd rather he got it off his chest than bottle it up, because if he bottles it up too much he may do injury to himself or to somebody else.

'If the inmate has enough respect for a certain officer to feel that he can tell him about problems at home, then that is a credit to the officer concerned. The officer needs to have genuine sympathy and even charity; it doesn't matter, for example, how badly an inmate has treated his family – in the sense that he's continually committed crimes and got himself back into prison, divorcing himself from his responsibilities – whatever the reasons for that, the officer has to forget them during the time that he's talking to the inmate.'

The question of the prison officer's role in prisoners' welfare is likely to remain unresolved for some time yet, for the welfare officer brings to his relationship with the prisoner an essential ingredient which the prison officer can never possess: disinterest. Furthermore, prison officers belong to a working group which insists on maintaining a division between work and leisure; if he works an extra hour he expects to be paid for doing so.

In a better world more prison officers would share Mr Hull's idealism. I saw traces of it elsewhere, but the general emphasis on control and security – with a concomitant stress on discipline – leaves small breathing space for more than the basic human concern. It is in the nature of the prison officer's task to regard the other as object.

Even the idealist failed to unravel the contradictions inherent in a system whose cornerstone is discipline, whose most insistent demand is that its subjects adjust to the rules of the regime which governs them, on pain of punishment – ultimately horrible punishments – for failing to do so. Mr Hull would like to have seen the introduction of a reward system, whereby prisoners earn their privileges.

'A man who is not toeing the line, who is creating problems for the authorities, who won't settle in, should only be able to receive some forms of privileges if he works hard towards them, by acting in a reasonable, adult manner. I want him to be of the frame of mind in which he says to himself: Right, it's up to me, I've got to behave myself, abide by the rules of the establishment, and then I know that I'll be given something because I've earned it.'

This seems like common sense, but there is little logic in the idea of adjustment to a punitive regime as preparation for a fit re-entry into free society. The principle implies that a man will not be allowed to return to society until he has learned to adjust to prison.

At social occasions prison officers talked about their own hardships, their disagreements with governors' policies or with social workers, their shooting clubs and their overtime, but never specifically about their charges. Some of them also complained that people like me had our priorities wrong.

'The reason I wanted to have a chat with you', Pete Thomson, a burly authoritarian man, said to me in a bar one night at an officer's leaving party, 'is that in books about prisons people always take the con's side and never think about the prison officer. You've got psychologists, social workers, lawyers, all working for them – but one day the British public is going to wake up to the fact that there are hundreds of men in prison in this country for murdering and raping and stealing, who're there for no other reason than that they like doing it.'

Pete had come into the service from the navy at the same time as Tommy Wilson, a Scotsman; they had gone through their training together and been in the same job at Lewes for thirteen years. They were also members of the same shooting club. Pete was a natural candidate for the MUFTI course which had recently taken place at Lewes. (MUFTI – minimum use of force tactical intervention – is a system under which officers are trained to control violent incidents of 'concerted indiscipline'; according to the *Report on the work of the Prison Department*, 1983, 'MUFTI will be used only when other methods of restoring order have failed'.) Tommy, on the other hand, had declined the offer to take part in the course. He wouldn't do it, he said. I asked why not.

'I'd need to be sure I wasn't going to be prosecuted afterwards if I hit somebody too hard, or if I killed someone. If you go into a situation such as that training is designed for, there's no use giving a little hit here and little hit there, as the Home Office suggests; you have to get the adrenalin going, don't you? You have to get wound up a bit, give it a hundred per cent. If they give me a stick and put me in the front line and then some fellow comes at me waving a broken half of a strip of neon light, I'm not going to tap him politely on a vulnerable spot, am I? No, I would need to have it down in black and white that I wasn't going to be prosecuted for that kind of thing.'

Then, chuckling naughtily, he told a story which illustrates that brutality need not be physical. It was about an assistant governor at another prison who refused to communicate directly with prisoners.

'What? Speak with inmates? We have uniformed men to do that sort of thing!'

On the occasions when it was necessary to confront prisoners – such as at the daily adjudications – he would sit behind the desk with a principal officer by his side. The officer would relay the Assistant Governor's questions to the prisoner and the prisoner's replies back to the Assistant Governor. A typical conversation might go like this:

'Sir, may I ask a question?'

'The prisoner wishes to know if he may ask a question, sir.'

'Yes.'

'Sir, is it still allowed to have my extra weekly letter, paid for out of my prison wages, while doing time in the block?'

'The prisoner wishes to know if, while serving a period of cellular confinement in the segregation unit, he is permitted to retain the privilege of the canteen letter.'

'Certainly not.'

'The Assistant Governor says no.'

14 Nicked

The prisoner is placed on report, nicked, and is subject to internal discipline. The charge is drawn from Rule 47 of the Prison Rules (1964),
which states that 'A prisoner shall be guilty of an offence against discipline'
if he:

   1) mutinies or incites another prisoner to mutiny;
   2) does gross personal violence to an officer;
   3) does gross personal violence to any person not being an officer;
   4) commits any assault. . . .

The list continues for twenty-one paragraphs, prepared for a multitude of
sins. Paragraph 14: 'uses any abusive, insolent, threatening or other improper language'; paragraph 15: 'is indecent in language, act or gesture'. In
case of unforeseen omission, paragraph 20 states, 'in any way offends
against good order and discipline'.

   Some prisoners go through long sentences without ever getting nicked.
For others it is a regular, even a more or less weekly occurrence. After the
officer has filled out the report form, giving details of the alleged offence,
the prisoner is served with a copy – a 'telegram' – and told that he will be
appearing before an adjudication hearing next morning. If the offence is a
serious one – for instance, if he is held to be causing continual disruption
on the wing – he will be held overnight in the Segregation Unit, formerly
called the punishment block, known simply as the block. A random sample
of charges ranges from the trivial – having an unlisted or improperly listed
radio, swearing at an officer or refusing to work – to the serious, such as
planning an escape or assaulting an officer.

   Adjudications are presided over by the Governor, his deputy or one of
his assistant governors. They take place every morning in a room adjacent
to the Segregation Unit. It isn't really a room at all, but a broad vaulted
passageway between two doors, in which has been installed a desk and
some chairs, and a mat for the acccused to stand on. Its anomalous nature
makes it an uncomfortable place to stay for long: low ceiling, close walls,
the lack of accustomed definition; it is like being in the upper half of a
barrel.

The presiding governor (an assistant, in this case) enters the adjudications room and sits down behind the desk, followed by the Chief Officer, who sits on his left-hand side. They exchange a few words regarding procedure. Once settled, the governor calls to the two attendant officers waiting at the door which links the room to the block, 'Right, bring in the prisoner.'

The two officers lead him from a Segregation cell where he will either have been kept overnight, or, having been brought down from the wing, held until his trial began; in this case, the prisoner was doing a spell in the block already when he allegedly offended. They position the prisoner on the mat before the governor, then take up station between the prisoner and the governor's desk at an oblique angle, facing the prisoner, in case he should leap at his judge across the floor. Next, the officer responsible for placing him on report, Mr O'Leary, comes and stands at the desk on the governor's right, while the Senior Officer in charge of administering the Segregation Unit, Mr Carrol, stands behind the prisoner at the back of the room.

His name is Hill. He is about twenty years old, tall and thin and gangly, not yet properly physically developed, black, with teeth missing. When he speaks his speech is incoherent, as if he has never learned how to manage the relationships between lips, teeth and tongue. He is unconvicted by the courts of any offence and is being kept in the wing for young prisoners, A Wing, on remand awaiting trial.

With some attempt at ceremony, Mr O'Leary straightens his shoulders, puts his chin in the air, and reads out the charge.

Rule 47, paragraph 14: 'The prisoner shall be guilty of an offence against discipline if he . . . uses any abusive, insolent, threatening or other improper language.' Mr O'Leary, a youngish man with a friendly face, reads his evidence from a prepared statement: Hill's shirt was unbuttoned when he was unlocked in the morning for slopping out; when Mr O'Leary told him to smarten himself up, he abused the officer, was 'truculent' and 'insolent'.

Hill is asked by the governor if he wishes to question Mr O'Leary's version of events; he shakes his head and mumbles that he does not. Then he is allowed to give his own version of what happened, which differs only in emphasis from that of Mr O'Leary. Hill pleads mitigation on account of the excessive heat in his cell – which he hopes will explain his unbuttoned shirt. The governor looks impassive as Hill blurts out his inarticulate plea. Mr O'Leary speaks up to say that this is not the first time Hill has been 'truculent' – a word he is fond of – and that he has been warned before of

the need to maintain a smart appearance and to obey disciplinary procedure, especially while serving time in the Segregation Unit. His shirt is
frequently unbuttoned and hanging out of his trousers, Mr O'Leary says,
and his general appearance is always sloppy.

The governor nods. 'How do you plead, Hill?' he asks.

'Guilty.'

'Guilty, *sir*,' mumbles Mr Carrol from behind.

'Guilty, sir,' he repeats, barely audible.

Then the governor turns to the Chief, who has been watching the
proceedings with a stern gaze which has never left the prisoner. The Chief
has Hill's file open before him on the desk, and he begins to leaf through it.

'What do we know about him, Chief?'

The record is bad. Hill's behaviour has been consistently mutinous, he
has been placed on report several times since being imprisoned on remand
five months earlier, and is currently serving three days' cellular confinement for abusing an officer on the wing. The 'three days' – the
maximum a prison governor can impose at a time – is a formality in his
case; Hill's spells tend to run into each other.

While the Assistant Governor and the Chief Officer conferred over the
bad record, Hill, standing between the two officers, raised his eyes to the
ceiling; he was smiling, as if he knew something the others did not. Then
his head shook slightly, and went on shaking until the shaking became a
lolling from side to side, and all the while he smiled. He seemed to have
something to say which could not be spoken – not that he hadn't been
offered the opportunity by the governor to reply to Mr O'Leary's charges
against him, as the rules state he must be, but that the words of the
governor, the Chief, Mr Carrol and Mr O'Leary comprised a language he
did not share – though he might have understood each word individually –
as they did not share his. He was dumb and they did not understand the
signs he made. They understood it when he asked for mitigation (without
using that word) but his plea was really only a few phrases he had learned
to stammer out in their tongue, cobbled together like restaurant-French for
the sake of getting by in practical matters. That was not what he wished to
communicate, which was done by signs. They actively charged him with
making those signs, however; and the more signs, the more punishment.

Hill's big round head, with its uneven rows of teeth and tufty black hair
and big stage-darkie eyes, lolled around in the air while the Chief and the
governor sternly discussed this breach of the rules and that offence against
good order and discipline. Meanwhile, Mr O'Leary scrutinized the prisoner's

behaviour and shook his own head disgustedly, regarding what he saw as greater vindication of his own action, and as one more stage towards the inexorable expression of Hill's incipient madness.

It was a queer pantomine and it seemed to go on for a long time: the murmuring Chief, the lolling head, the contemptuous stare of Mr O'Leary.

Finally, the governor looked up and turned his attention back to the prisoner, and as he spoke the half-barrelled room regained a semblance of normality. It was as if all the furniture had been floating around in the air without anyone noticing except Hill and now it had silently landed on the floor again.

'Right, Hill,' said the governor, 'I find you guilty as charged. You have abused an officer, contrary to the rules of discipline, and you'll have to be punished for it. You'll have to give yourself a shake, Hill, you're in prison now and you can't expect to play around and get away with it every time. You've been warned before about your appearance and haven't taken any notice, and that's why you find yourself here. I sentence you to another three days' cellular confinement, with total loss of privileges, and seven days' prospective loss of remission.'

Three days' solitary confinement and seven days' loss of remission – for an argument over tucking in a shirt! 'You're in prison now,' the Assistant Governor had said, but Hill was unconvicted of any offence. The governor was not being especially harsh by himself, he was merely apeing the system of which he was part and which was part of him. The qualification 'prospective' had to be added to the sentence of loss of remission, because Hill was untried and therefore not serving a sentence from which seven days of his automatic remission could be subtracted. Loss of privileges means that his bed will be taken out of his cell from seven in the morning till seven at night, and that books, extra baths, and all other luxuries will be withdrawn.

The governor closed the file in front of him to signify an end to the trial, and the prisoner, his face again blank, was led away by the two officers who guarded the governor against him throughout the performance. Everyone else stood up and returned to their duties.

I was last out. I walked down the corridor, alongside the row of cell doors, from the adjudications room to the exit from the block. Only half a minute had passed since proceedings in the curious little half-room had terminated, but there was no sign of Hill or his two jailers, and no sound except that of my own footsteps and of the officer who was to let me out.

The block is below ground level, with tiny windows only on the cell side;

the plaster has peeled, leaving large white areas on wall and ceiling, and damp has soiled much of the rest. The ceiling is imposing, and the cell doors are so low that prisoners have to stoop whenever they walk in or out. Only the strip lighting overhead saves the place from parodying a gothic dungeon.

It is hard to imagine, now, only seconds after the little theatre in which Hill mimed his part has ended, that these low doors shield heads lolling in the air, faces approaching expression, eyes searching for something to look at, tongues dumb and getting dumber. Only the regiment of folded beds, each one opposite its sleeper's door in the corridor, gives the lie to a total absence of population.

Hill's signs could not be understood by anyone else — were, in fact, incommunicable. Yet they represented the deepest contact with his inner self that he was capable of achieving. He was a remand, living among boys, had been in prison only five months. Gradually, he would adopt a more traditional tried and tested method of reacting to the stern gaze and disgusted scrutiny coming from the uniform, and would learn how to make his response coherent in their grammar. And at the same time he would unlearn the signs and syllables of his own language, which had baffled them.

15 The Block

STATEMENT OF EVIDENCE   HMP A—
REPORTING OFFICER (NAME AND RANK)   Smithies. Officer. J.M.
RELATING TO THE CHARGES UNDER RULE 47 (PARA(S)): 4

REPORT

Sir, At approximately 08.00 hrs on the 2.11.83 in the Segregation Unit I unlocked Cell 3 which was occupied by 2113 MacDonald so that he could slop out, as I opened his cell door I noticed that he had spread excreta over himself and the walls of his cell, I immediately closed the door of the cell.

At approximately 08.30 hrs after we had slopped out and fed the other inmates in the Segregation Unit I went to MacDonald's cell in the company of officer Andrews and others we were dressed in protective clothing. As we unlocked his door MacDonald was standing with his back to the wall holding a chamber pot full of liquid and other matter. As we entered his cell he threw the pot at us the contents of which went over myself and officer Andrews. MacDonald was then removed to special cell 1. The minimum use of force necessary was used.

Officer Smithies. J.M.

REPORT

Sir, At approximately 08.30 hours on the 2.11.83 I was in the Segregation Unit assisting other officers to restrain 2113 MacDonald and to relocate him in special cell 1.

As I was attempting to pick up his legs, MacDonald kicked out at me hitting me in the stomach area with his foot. The force he used was such that I fell back and injured my back resulting in me having to report sick and go off duty. This is my evidence.

Officer Polsdon, T.K.

STATEMENT OF WITNESS

STATEMENT OF:	T. McCabe
AGE OF WITNESS:	Over 21
OCCUPATION OF WITNESS:	Medical Practitioner

I examined MacDonald at HM Prison B—on 16 November 1983 . . . I noticed a
fading bruise with a yellow tinge one inch in diameter on the lateral aspect of the
right upper arm. There was also an even less distinct bruise one and half inches in
diameter above the tip of the right shoulder. Some tenderness was noted of the
muscles in this area namely of the right deltoid and right trapezium muscle.

Pink healing abrasions two inches ¾ were noted over the lumbar spine. No
bruising was evident over the thighs although he had some pain in this area.

I felt that the bruising abrasions and muscle tenderness were consistent with an
incident occuring approximately two weeks previously. His general condition at the
time was extremely good and during the period in this prison he has always shown a
cheerful frame of mind.

I had the opportunity of examining him again on the 26 March 1984 and all
bruising, abrasions and tenderness have gone and he remains symptom free.

Benny MacDonald attempted to start criminal proceedings against the
prison officers who had removed him to 'special cell 1' in A—Prison with
'the minimum use of force necessary', resulting in the injuries which Dr
McCabe inspected two weeks after their infliction. The Chief Superintendent to whom he made his complaint, however, replied that in the
opinion of the DPP there was 'insufficient evidence to justify proceedings
against any Prison Officer'. There was more of a case to be made for
bringing charges against Benny MacDonald, the Superintendent wrote, 'in
re. of the injury sustained by Mr Smithies', and also by Mr Polsdon.

Benny had his fight in one prison, his medical inspection in another, and
received his reply from the police in yet another, not by any means the last
in which he would sit out the remainder of his three-year sentence for
burglary. (His bad behaviour had deprived him of all remission.)

When I met Benny, in the punishment block in Lewes, he had served
exactly two years; indeed, the day we met was the day when he would have
been released, had he kept all his remission for good behaviour. Benny was
reminded of this while we were talking, much as he might have remembered an appointment he should have kept with the optician, and he
showed no regret at having missed it. When prison is an involuntary but
accepted part of your life, three is only a little different from two.

Lewes was the fifteenth prison he had been in during these two years; he
had seen the Segregation Unit in all of them, and the 'special cell' –

isolation cells, with padded walls, multiple doors, no windows, constant electric lights and no furniture – in more than one.

His latest bit of internal trouble started after a rooftop protest at Lewes. It was staged as a protest against being moved out of C—Prison, where he had been before coming here. Benny claimed to have been happy in C—, and to have settled down to serve out the rest of his sentence peacefully. He made friends with three fellow Scotsmen and with them developed the sort of camaraderie which only Glaswegians from his type of female-exclusive, male-oriented society can.

After he had been in C—Prison for six weeks, however, someone posted a note to the prison officers about Benny and his friends in the letter box on the wing, and on a December morning in 1984 Benny was put on a ghost train which eventually arrived at Lewes (though he wasn't told so on the journey, receiving only the standard reply in answer.to his enquiries: 'You'll find out when you get there').

Eight days after his arrival at Lewes, he wrote a vivid account of his removal from his previous prison, given here complete with the author's markings.

'At 6.30 a.m. on the morning of the 6th December 1984, I was fast asleep only to be made very awake by the shout's of "your on the way out", I was still in bed for I was pinned there by numerous officer's, I was handcuffed to two officer's whilst still in bed naked except for a shirt "which I had slept in" I was then systematically punched and kicked about the body, whilst this brutal attack was being made on me I heard other scream's and shout's from near by, "I was to find out 'shortly' afterwards" that these screams etc: were made by 3 of my very good friends who were also being attacked and removed in roughly the same fashion as I, however whilst still in my own cell, under a barrage of kick's punches and abuse, one of the officers in my cell "a senior officer" [. . .] shouted to somebody "outside my cell" that leg-straps were needed for me, when I heard this I stopped struggling. "I was basically attempting to defend myself, during a brutal attack" I shouted to the officer's that, if they stopped hitting me, and put on my trousers I would "walk" out, they eventually cooled down enough and put on my trousers "remember I'm still cuffed to two officers" and was therefore unable to put my own trousers on, once my trousers and shoes were on I then was dragged half carried out of my cell. It was then that I saw a friend of mine "Davy Jones" being carried down the stairs surrounded by numerous officer's. I saw one of these officers "who I do not know by name" punch Davy in the face region, I immediately started to struggle and shout at them to leave him alone, "I had a good view of what was happening to Davy" for I was at the top landing and he was going down steps carried bodily, by as I said before "numerous" officers. I believe Davy was naked and in Leg-Straps (I later saw him outside the wing being carried into one of 4 vans that were present). I also heard earlier the shouts of my other friend Johnny MacInnes. He was also I believe to have been under attack, though I never saw Johnny the whole time! However I did see past "Shuggie Dougan's" cell "which is about 4 or 5 doors away from mine" that Shuggie was on the floor "naked" and surrounded by officers who were kicking him, I believe they had put Leg-Straps on Shuggie also! After seeing Davy and Shuggie I was obviously very angry and upset and I therefore continued to struggle and shout leave them alone although this just made the officers attached and surrounding me violent towards me once more therefore I stopped struggling. As I was leaving the wing I saw Davy being carried into one of the prison vans "he was screaming for them to stop hitting him and shouting leave me alone". I once again got very upset and started struggling and shouting at the officers "what are you doing to my mate". During this struggle by me I was again attacked, I was grabbed round the throat by a senior officer and I nearly lost consciousness. I felt as if I was going to faint. He had me round the throat for what seemed an eternity, though it must have been a matter of seconds. I obviously stopped struggling and became passive once more and was put into the van still handcuffed to two officers who had also struck out at me during the whole incident. Whilst sitting in the van I felt cold and weak and very frightened. I could see Davy in one of the other vans. He was handcuffed to the bars of the windows. There was about 5 officers sitting opposite him. Davy looked totally dejected and shattered. I did not see "Shuggie Dougan" being carried out into his van, nor did I see little Johnny MacInnes being put into one "though I knew by now" that all four of us, me, Davy Jones, Shuggie, and Johnny MacInnes were being *moved*. "It was obvious to me even before I noticed there was 4 prison vans" because of what I had earlier seen and heard.

At one stage in all the commotion one of my escorts shouted "we've had enough of you Scottish bastards", (excuse the language) all 4 of us are Scottish born and bred "and proud of it".

I was well and truly shocked by the whole incident "it was so unexpected" and unprovoked, we had all been settling down in C—after our past troubles with the system, we kept ourselves to ourselves, we never bothered *no-body*. I believe we did nothing as individuals or in a group to merit such treatment as was meted out to us at C—, the transfer on its own would have been sufficient in shocking me as I know we had been settled there and caused no trouble.

We left the prison in a convoy of 4 prison vans (green in colour). Once outside the prison gates we were accompanied by a police escort with flashing lights. It stayed at the front of the convoy. (The police escort I thought was an over reaction by the authorities and needless, especially when all 4 of us are serving relatively short sentences and are all Ct-B.)

My van departed from the others some miles away from the prison, and we "broke down". At this stage I made the *mistake* of asking where I was going, and why, and what all the trouble was about, for needless to say this started an argument and therefore I received a slap in the face and had my hair pulled back by the senior officer. This unprovoked attack by the escort on me ended after about 30 seconds. Up until now [the senior officer] had been responsible for hitting me once in the cell, once outside the cell, and outside the wing when he tried to throttle me, other officers including the 2 I was handcuffed to had assaulted me previously, unfortunately I do not know their names. After this incident in the van (which was at this stage parked on the hard shoulder) it must have been a matter of minutes before 3 police cars and one policevan (meat wagon) came on the scene. I was then removed from the prison van and placed into the police van still attached to my two *brutal* prison officers, (I received quite a bit of verbal abuse from a police sergeant as I was being put into the police van) I was in great shock, I couldn't understand why all this happening to me, for I felt that I had done nothing to merit the violence nor the transfer.

However, once in the van (police van) in the company of the 2 prison officers attached to me as well as [the] senior officer and a principal officer and 2 police officers, we were on the move again. We were escorted by 3 police cars "one behind us, one in front and one just to the right of us" with once again flashing lights, I overheard one of the policemen saying that we were going to Crawley Police Station. We got to Crawley Police Station without further incident, I had remained very passive since the last incident in the prison van. I feared further violence.

At the station I was taken to the cell "there was a large number of police officers present as well as the 4 prison officers. I was threatened before the handcuffs were removed that if I got *stroppy* I would be DONE. This threat came from a police officer! I remained silent, had the handcuffs removed and was placed in a very small cell.

I was at Crawley for about 1 hour before I again was cuffed to the same two prison officers as before and taken to another prison van. I was in the van with the same 4 officers as before and driver, we then set off again "with a police escort" ahead of us all the way to Lewes prison. I did not want any more violence or abuse from the officers so I remained silent all the way to the prison and apart from the odd bit of abuse by my escort on me I remained free of any violence on this part of my journey.

I felt pretty weak, my throat was still sore, and my back and legs and my side were aching.

However, we arrived at Lewes prison, I was taken straight to reception, handcuffs were removed and my escort disappeared somewhere and I was put into a small waiting room. I did not make any complaints to the doctor or staff because of past experience in these type of situations. I knew that complaint would be useless. I had by now decided that I would be protesting in the near future in one way or another for the way me and my 3 friends were treated, I did not have any apparent bruising on my body after close inspection by myself later, though I did feel rather sore and weak. All I had were the aches and the memory! I was well and truly dejected and sad and bitter at the whole episode. I was placed in the Segregation Unit here at Lewes Prison where I stayed over night until the following morning. I was then placed on normal location on C-Wing "Still at this stage not knowing where my friends were."'

Benny was bad about times. He had spent a large proportion of the two years he had served of his sentence in solitary, and when I first met him he had been in the block at Lewes for eight weeks. That was a figure he would have been incapable of supplying by himself, however. He would refer to an incident 'a couple of weeks back', which, it would later emerge, had happened three months ago; and he was equally likely to telescope time the other way, mistaking weeks for months.

Solitary confinement is a hallucinogen, a destroyer of objectivity and a producer of paranoia. The victim hears sounds and interprets them according to his own fantasies, ornamenting them with the hidden motives of his enemies; he adorns the silences with his private music, and papers over the abyss of time which faces him, either with a neurotic circumspection regarding routine or else with a blanket which, in effect, removes the progressive concept of time as a movement which brings changes. He trusts no one. Even the prisoner next door (if there is one: sometimes prisoners are separated by empty cells), with whom he communicates furtively through the window, comes under periodic suspicion. He could be a spy, he could be executing some mysterious plot of his own, he could be a poisoner, he could be mad; he could be all of these.

All of this Benny suffered, although he appeared constitutionally strong enough to withstand its worst effects. The 'cheerful frame of mind' remarked on by the doctor who inspected him for a fortnight after his spot of bother at A—was one of the most extraordinary things in the prison.

The Senior Officer in charge of the block was Mr Carrol. He occupied a small office, converted out of a cell, halfway along the underground corridor, giving him a central position in the T-shaped block. It was early afternoon when I entered and a winter sun was shining outside, but the block is always artificially lighted.

Mr Carrol gave me a quick summary of the routine for a prisoner being held 'in seg'. There are basically two sorts: those being held in the interests of 'good order and discipline' and those who are segregated for their own protection – sometimes by request, sometimes not – usually informers and sex offenders, for the most part involving minors. The different factions are not supposed to come into contact at any time. Meals are dished out to one lot while the other is still locked up; exercise is taken in isolation; cleaning tasks – always performed by a prisoner – are performed when no one else is around. The justification is 'control', but the effect is punishment.

On the first day that I was there, there were thirteen residents; six young prisoners (all on remand) and seven adults, with a majority being held for good order and discipline. They rise at 6.30, slop out and wash, and have breakfast. Then there is half an hour's exercise, and with that the day's activity is more or less over, punctuated thereafter only by mealtimes. For the 43s there is cleaning or cell work – stamping letters for the censors, sewing on buttons – but for those on punishment there is none. Baths and books are awarded and withdrawn at the Senior Officer's discretion, all, supposedly, in the interests of control.

The average length of stay in the block is from three to seven days. The maximum a prison governor can mete out at a time is three, but the independent Board of Visitors may award up to twenty-eight days, always renewable.

Mr Carrol showed me the Register of Offenders under Punishment: a record (kept for eight years) of individuals' baths and exercise periods, and also of observation. A typical entry for the latter reads like this:

3.30: asleep
3.45: asleep
4.00: pacing cell
4.15: laying down
4.30: sitting in chair
4.45: sitting in chair
5.00: pacing cell

(The same type of watch is kept, in the hospital, on 'suicide risks', who are otherwise left alone with their potential murderers.) Another, unofficial log gives information on the prisoner's attitude and behaviour during time spent in the Segregation Unit: 'insolent', 'cheerful', 'uncooperative' and so on.

Asleep, pacing cell, lying down, sitting in chair, ditto, ditto, ditto; rise, wash, slop out, breakfast, exercise. . . . The routine is essential anywhere in the prison as a way of establishing a rhythm, of keeping time and therefore keeping sanity. In the block, however, it is actually a system of metaphysics – the subject's primary method of confirming his being.

Mr Carrol had no objection to letting me see MacDonald, although he recommended instead the block's other long-server – much longer, indeed, than Benny – who had been in for eighteen months and showed no signs of coming out. This was 'Old Kerr', a lifer protesting his innocence. But I preferred to be introduced to MacDonald. I had been meaning for some time to find out what was behind the rooftop protest. Mr Carrol shrugged and said okay. He thought MacDonald was a troublemaker.

He led me to a short row of cells, behind another gate, ranged along one side of the vertical leg of the T. The doors are only a little over five foot high, cut into thick walls. Mr Carrol unlocked the door of the cell and swung it open. (I had to restrain an impulse to ask him to knock first.) The prisoner had been lying on his bed but sat up at the sound of the key, looking at first alarmed at the unexpected sight of a visitor.

What should my approach be? Not to smile too willingly, extend a hand too ingratiatingly, but also to be wary of appearing stern and official. The atmosphere was charged with suspicion. I was conscious of feeling too smartly dressed – though I wasn't particularly – of the raincoat draped over my arm and the tape recorder in my hand. The prisoner stood up from the bed and approached us.

'This is James Cameron,' said the Senior Officer. 'This here's MacDonald. Don't know his first name.'

We shook hands. He smiled. The Senior Officer left us alone.

Benny – 'He knows my first name all right' – pointed to the chair and sat himself on the edge of the bed. In the block the tables and chairs are made from thick, corrugated cardboard interlocking pieces. The chair doesn't feel like a real chair. The table looks like an upturned box. Officially, strategically, this is to prevent them being used as weapons or barricades – Mr Carrol was of the opinion that such furniture should be installed in the cells on the wings as well – but it also contributes to the solitary prisoner's sense of disorientation, of imbalance, to the distortion of the perceptible world. Deprived already of a proper sense of time, he is also disallowed the certainty of the things he touches, sits upon, writes, reads and eats at, being what they appear to be – which in turn affects each of these activities accordingly. The aim is consistent with the original objectives of the Pentonville experiment almost a century and a half ago: to 'soften the affections', although the object is no longer to instil a sense of Godfearing dread with a view to reformation of the soul; nowadays it is merely in the interests of control.

Those on 'cellular confinement' have their beds taken out of their cells between the hours of seven and seven, and are forced to use the non-chair or else stand up, pace the cell or lie on the floor.

Benny, however, did not fall into this category. He was in the block awaiting a hearing before the Board of Visitors, following his rooftop protest against being forcibly and involuntarily removed from his previous prison. Until that hearing took place, he refused to work or cooperate with the regime in any other way. Mr Carrol was in some way justified, then, in saying that he was in the block by choice. As such, he was permitted a full set of privileges: an hour's exercise, often taken with the prisoner next door (an unusual privilege for which he was grateful), three baths a week, newspapers and books. His current reading included the Bible, psychology and thrillers.

His interest in psychology sprang from a desire to make some sense of his miserable background and upbringing in Glasgow. Born in a slum on the south side of the city, Benny had started stealing early and was placed in the care of a Home by his drunken father at the age of nine. Since then he had trod the familiar path from detention centre to borstal to prison, staying out of trouble only for months at a time, and within the prison, from the wing to the block to the special cell, eventually being belted up in a straitjacket and leg straps.

His next experience of family life had not turned out to be much better. He had a girl whom he called his wife, Kay, and with her he had a child. He showed me photographs. The child was his greatest pride – he told me so but it was obvious. There was one picture of the little boy standing by a river, turning to face the camera, a colour photograph snapped on a Polaroid camera of the type which produces instant results. The boy had blonde curls and his father's cheek.

Then he showed me a letter he had lately received from Kay.

> Benny,
>   Please don't write to me any more.
>   I don't really know how to tell you, but I suppose I've just got to put it straight.
>   I'm married now. . . . Sorry.
>   Kay XX
> PS: I did it for the kids sake

'Not a very nice letter to get in a place like this,' he said, putting it away among his files. A master of understatement, Benny.

He was twenty-four and this was his third prison sentence, although he had lost count of the number of spells in youth custody institutions. It wasn't the fault of the authorities that he was in the block, as he admitted; he had opted for it. Prison was an extension of the world he had been born into and just as he had got his own back on that one by stealing to hurt his father, so now he was getting his own back on this by protests such as the rooftop one.

I could see that he would forever be engaged in getting his own back, unless he one day succeeded in breaking free by force of an act comparable to the leap of faith experienced by religious converts. The system's proclaimed methods for controlling the likes of Benny are not only futile but counter-productive, since he will always react more and not less violently to violence.

The doors on the special cell are reinforced and multiplied, body belts and leg straps are put on – but nothing, except death, is stronger than his will, and so the stronger they make the doors and the belts the greater he discovers his resources of power to be.

One hears prison authorities talk about 'violent men, *very* violent men', as if prison and its methods had no part in making the man so very, very violent – blind, apparently, to the role of constant light, triple steel doors, isolation, silence and 'sensory deprivation' in bringing him to this threshold.

The rooftop protest itself was a comparatively mild affair. At just before two o'clock on 11 December – three days after his arrival at Lewes – during the exercise period for prisoners on normal location, he had climbed on to the roof of the paints workshop which is close to the yard. The officer in charge, seeing him moving from one end of the roof to the other, quickly herded up the rest of the men, drove them back inside and blew his whistle for assistance. Benny had taken up his position at the extreme end of the roof so that, as he said, 'When they come up after you they know that if you fall off they go with you.'

Out of respect for his decent reception at Lewes, compared with what he had experienced elsewhere, Benny had decided in advance to make his protest a peaceful one. He could, after all, he said, have torn up the slates and thrown them to the ground. Instead, he merely waited until satisfied that the reason behind his protest had been transmitted to all whose task it was to entice him down and who would be reporting on it later. After having been up for four hours, he demanded the presence of a member of the Board of Visitors (who bravely climbed on to the roof to identify himself by means of his card) and then came down. He had been given promises of a bath, a meal and a fair hearing, which were kept. The Governor in his report, Benny said, had written a clear account of what had happened during the protest and the reasons which lay behind it.

The protest had drawn attention to his complaint, he was to have a full hearing, with legal representation before the Board of Visitors, and would probably be on the move to another prison before long. Thus he had succeeded in his aim of putting a spoke, albeit a tiny one, in the wheels of the system and disrupting it a little.

He felt that it had been worth it. I felt, though I would have found it difficult to say so to Benny, that it was pointless, that he could fairly be described as 'a troublemaker' – though a very likeable one – that his claims to have caused 'no aggravation' for the authorities at this prison revealed an astonishing self-centredness, and that his just proposal to behave as he was treated, if he was serious about it, had to start with him.

But I could also see that these counter-arguments were shortsighted and only produced further counter-arguments. Although he may have started the endless cycle of behaving badly and being treated badly within the context of the prison system, he had not really started it, not in the beginning. A complex network involving family, society and education had done that. Whatever had happened to his soul during the early years leading to his being given away by his father, it had established a pattern, an inexorable development like that of a foetus in the womb, which resulted in the man now before me.

When Benny protested that he wanted to behave as he was treated he was really crying out against his birthright. He had been classified as uncontrollable by his family, which had handed over responsibility to society, which had then passed it on to the prison system – which too, however, had failed to make him adjust. This was the path which had led to his presence here in the block, a history of assaults on and by prison officers behind him: his world finally shrunk to four indescribably bare walls below ground level, with a cardboard table and chair.

A protest such as the rooftop one was crucial to his continuing sense of himself, it was his way of confirming that he had, after all, some worth in this wilderness, of making his voice heard and defeating the insufferable torment of remaining silent. Pointless it may have been but it was none the less a necessary act.

16 The Wall

He was the Security Officer, which meant that he was responsible, among other things, for making sure escapes did not occur. He also oversaw the admission of outsiders into the prison – whether they be press, local dignitaries or workmen – the surveillance of visitors and the methods used to detect smugglers, and the use of drugs or possession of weapons by prisoners on the wing.

It was his job to brief me formally before issuing me a pass. After making me sign a form with a set of rules concerning behaviour and providing me with a verbal run-down on the most important of the rules, and asking to be tipped the wink if I should happen to be made party to or hear about anything fishy – drug smuggling, illegal letters – Senior Officer Lorimer added a 'word of advice' of his own – 'after twenty-five years' experience':

'There are a hundred and fifty men in that wing: evil, perverted, 'orrible men – all of 'em. And you, to them, will be turkey-for-the-plucking.'

He was a small, wiry man, somewhat bleary-eyed and seldom without a cigarette, with silver hair over which he wore his hat cocked at a cheeky angle. He was called Lorry and was well liked among colleagues; at a party in a pub to celebrate his retirement some months later, the bar was packed with well-wishers and speech-makers, merrily, though regretfully, seeing old Lorry exchange his prison key for a lollipop-man's stick.

'The problem here, and I make no bones about it, is the Governor. He is nominally in charge of security, but he has delegated that responsibility to his Deputy. Now, from my point of view, this could hold up an important operation, because occasionally I have to ask for ratification from the Dep, who, if it's a delicate business, feels obliged to say, "Oh, I'd better talk to the Governor about this." All right, but where the hell is the Governor? He's not in his office, is he? Now, already five minutes have been wasted in relaying messages backwards and forwards between various offices trying to find the bloody Governor. Five minutes that could be crucial to the success of an operation. Five minutes that could become fifteen, or even fifty – in which case, forget it.'

In trying to prevent the flow of drugs or anything else illegal into the prison, the Security Officer had a difficult job. For 'drugs' read hashish or cannabis – 'puff'. There is a little heroin, which will probably increase, and some pills, which, though a few years ago the most popular drugs in prison, are decreasing in use. This at least is heartening, since hash is less harmful than any kind of uppers and downers. The Security Officer's concern, however, is less with prisoners' physical welfare – let the doctor look after that – than with the law.

Drugs come in through the visitors' room. A prisoner with good connections will be capable of scanning the visitors' list which is pinned up outside the wing office each day and reading it like racing form: Ah, MacDermott's got a visit today, that's a likely bet; Burnett – an utter certainty!

Dealing is carried on with cash, which itself is almost as coveted among prisoners as drugs. The amount of cash floating on the wing at any given time comes to about £200. A dealer who has had a lump of hash brought in can sell it in so-called 'half-ounce deals' (actually far lighter) for cash which he then uses, by way of his visitor contact, to purchase a larger amount, which again he sells once it arrives. Logically speaking, then, he can in this way accumulate all of the cash, or the main portion of it, within the prison, which bestows considerable power upon him in seeking other privileges and favours.

Everyone, including the Security Officer, knows about it, and no one seems able to stop it, short of strip-searching all visitors (most of whom are grandmothers, mothers, wives and children) and introducing separated visits behind glass screens. Such measures would not only be degrading but would inevitably lead to trouble, whereas it is the opinion of most prisoners, and some prison officers, that 'puff' helps to smother the latent seeds of revolt.

In so Lorimer's office, above the main gate, there were illustrations on the walls of possible smuggling tricks. One, captioned 'Things are not always what they seem', showed how a knife might be hidden in the buckle of a belt, another the way in which paper money could be kept inside a tobacco tin. Yet others suggested ways of finding out if a prisoner was taking drugs, beside which was a descriptive list of substances. Another wall had photographs of all the prisoners who held a security pass which enabled them to work outside the main block, or in the officers' mess. And there was also a list of the current escapees – 'E-risks' – from every prison in the land.

'This, as I am constantly reminding the Governor, is a Category B prison. But it's not like other Category B prisons. Usually you would have high perimeter security.' He used his fingers to enumerate: 'Prison dogs, electronic devices, high-mast lighting, alarms, TV cameras. . . . With the exception of the last, which we only succeeded in getting a few months ago, we don't have these things here.' This fact pleased some people, including the Governor, but not so Lorimer, whose main concern, after all, was with security, and ensuring that there were as few breaches of it as possible. 'It's a mickey mouse jail.'

Lorry Lorimer preferred the rigidity of Wandsworth, where he had worked for twelve years before being posted to Lewes. He stood up from his seat and turned his back on the fireplace, preparing to go through the old routine.

'In them days ninety-eight per cent of all officers would be ex-servicemen. The routine was like the navy. I'd unlock a man in the morning and I'd make him speak to me. I'd say "Good morning", and if there was no reply as I passed on to the next cell I'd take a step back and say, "You fuckin' deaf or something?' There'd always be a good morning after that. And if a con got cocky with me on the landing – you always get the type who's ready to show off in front of his mates – I'd just wait until it was lock-up time and then I'd go to his cell and say'—he hitched up his shoulders as if even then confronted by a recalcitrant captive – '"Right, what's it all about then?" 'Cause he knows I'm fifty-strong at the back if the need should arise, and all he has to do to prove it is to say the wrong thing at that moment. But it seldom came to that. They'd usually find a polite word for old Lorry after that.'

Then the Security Officer stood to attention and began to mime the Wandsworth walk – wake-up, slop-out, breakfast – which was always performed speedily and efficiently. He barked the commands and clapped his hands on the emphases: 'Right, *next*! – Right, *next*! – Right, *next*!—', while on the other beat his arms, like a traffic-policeman's, suggested movements of regimented convicts, down this staircase, up that one, forward along the left-hand gallery, back along the right, as if he were out of the mickey mouse jail for good and back where discipline meant what it stood for and the rule book ruled supreme.

His record on escapes since coming to Lewes was a good one. Nevertheless, he would have preferred to hold a tighter rein. This attitude conflicted with that of the Governor, who encouraged an atmosphere of cooperation among captives and captors, in the hope of spreading a climate more tolerable to breathe in while awaiting the hour when it was no longer necessary to escape.

How many try?

so Lorimer answered the question obliquely (in fact he thought that everyone was trying, all the time; it was his job to think so). A certain type of prisoner is always on the lookout, he said.

'You particularly have to watch the con who is cooperative all the time, who is always amenable. "Oh, bit of dirt along the corridor there" – gets a broom – "I'll do it, gov'nor." Always trying to help, never any trouble, *never any trouble at all.* So much so that he becomes invisible. They're the worst sort.'

No one can count the number of plans that are worked out but never acted upon or even spoken of. Plots that are hatched by night are found to be stillborn by day. Others are skillfully planned, but stubbornly refuse to become more than talk. The prisoner schemes, organizes, calculates, dreams – but finds that the more he does so the less he can do to force his limbs into action. Yet other plots are put into operation (usually after little planning) but are abandoned, without having attracted unwanted attention, before the light over the wall is glimpsed.

so Lorimer, as a protector of that light, applied himself to his task meticulously. His dislike of the Governor was only an aspect of his perfectionism, which the Governor wantonly thwarted by deflecting the Security Officer's emphasis on security.

On a piece of paper pinned above his desk so Lorimer had typed himself a memo:

When the door slams and the keys are quiet there is time for reflection on the infinite possibilities of success.

The simplest object in the cell takes on the significance of life and death. The fragment of wire, the nail painfully extracted from the wooden frame of the bed. The smallest morsel of glass or metal. All can become instruments of precision studded with diamonds, in the mind of the escaper.

The escaper is the man who must never admit defeat. He is always ready to attempt the unknown and to achieve the impossible with the minimum of aid.

Escape is not only a technique but a philosophy.

Wasn't it strange, I reflected later, that so Lorimer, the liquidator of escapes and therefore of hopes, was one of the most popular of prison officers among the prisoners.

He told me a comical story about two prisoners who planned an escape through the hole made in a wall by the removal of a ventilator fan. With sheets knotted together they made their way in heavy rain to the south wall. One managed to hoist himself up without any trouble but wet sheets and wall defeated the other one. So the first came back down to help him, only to find, when he tried again, that now he was earthbound too. So they broke back into the kit room from which they had removed the ventilator fan, changed out of their wet clothing, and stealthily made their way back into the main part of the prison. They were caught next morning after a thorough investigation, following the discovery of the wet clothing they had discarded in the kit room.

Escapers who succeeded only in breaking back into the prison gave particular satisfaction to Lorry Lorimer. Others are more successful, however.

On my first visit to the prison I had indicated the wall and asked the Governor if escapes were common. Without hesitation he replied, 'No, none at all.'

This was true at the time, but about a week later I read in the newspaper that a man had broken out of Lewes Prison. He planned his escape, I discovered afterwards, by observing the regularity with which a large skip containing bags of rubbish was removed from the yard by a truck which came in from outside to collect it. It used to arrive at 11.15 each morning and leave ten minutes later. One day the prisoner, who worked outside in the yard as a cleaner, hid himself in a specially prepared den among the rubbish in the waiting skip. When the truck hauled it out, he went with it.

From that day forwards the timetable for picking up rubbish was irregular, but the prisoner was 'on his toes' for several weeks before being arrested in London.

When I put it to another prisoner that this respite was hardly worth the trouble, given that he would face a severe punishment after his almost certain recapture, he disagreed. That month or two, he said, would make whatever followed (not to mention what had gone before) more bearable; and then there was always the chance, albeit a slim one, of staying out.

Escape is an instinct, like hunger. Once the instinct has been awakened in the prisoner, he has no choice but to attempt to satisfy it, and will go ahead with his plans even when he knows there is virtually no chance of success, or when he has no notion where he will go or what he will do if he should happen to find himself over the wall. So Lorimer believed in the security system, rejecting the liberal nonsense that the tougher the system the stronger the will to escape.

Whichever is true in broad terms, the effect upon Gilbert was the latter. Ten years into a life sentence for the attempted murder of a policeman, he had just been informed that the parole board would not even consider another application from him for another ten years – after which the soonest he could hope for actual release would be yet another three years.

Gilbert was not well liked on the wing. One day somebody posted a letter in the mean little box on the twos, and that evening the burglars spun Gilbert's cell. They found a hacksaw blade hidden in the mattress and the bars on the window almost sawed through. A spin on another cell the same day resulted in a catch of live ammunition. The two discoveries – probably spuriously – were linked.

Gilbert was ghosted out and returned to Category A. He would be under constant supervision from now on, even during visits to the lavatory. As a proven escape risk, he would wear luminous patches on all his clothes. If ever he did succeed in getting out – a near impossibility given the number of eyes trained on him – he would glow in the dark.

The wall is not only a wall: it is a blind, a shade, a drape, a curtain, a parasol; it is anything which shuts out the light. The prisoner begins to feel it physically, as he would a blindfold.

A few of the cells on the upper landings have a view of the surrounding downs (constricted by the tall trees in front of the prison and by the rooftops of the town) but from most the outlook is only the wall.

It is not for nothing that in the punishment block the windows are high up, and that the block itself is always below ground level, so that you have to contort your neck in order to see anything at all. In the special cells, used to hold 'uncontrollable' prisoners, any windows there are made of glass so thick it is opaque, or distorting. The ways of the jailor have remained constant throughout history: after imprisoning the captive, shave his head then gouge out his eyes.

Simon the painter had tunnelled his way out of the darkness by creating a private, lonely window with a beautiful view; in another way, T.C. had done the same thing with his maps. Others dreamed of women, fast cars and gold buried under the floorboards or at the end of a rainbow.

When I get out I'm going to. . .
'go abroad
'write a book
'prove myself somehow
'give it all up
'start my own business
'sell my story to the papers
'kill that bastard. . . .'

When I am released into the blessed greenery beyond the wall my sight will be restored and I will be saved.

I paid no attention to what most prisoners said they were going to do when they got out, suspecting that they had, quite naturally, mistaken the date of release for the day of redemption. In my first few days inside I heard enough about fast cars, Swiss banks, family estates, hungry women and patient – but rich – business partners anywhere in the world from Saudi Arabia to Bethnal Green to make me steer clear of that brand of romance for good.

But there was another, more potent, realistic romance taking place beyond the wall, undeniable and closer to the heart than anything else: the domestic world of things; of women arranging households, children playing, couples taking trains and walking in open streets.

'Last night,' the captive hero in John Cheever's novel *Falconer* writes to a former girlfriend, 'watching a comedy on TV, I saw a woman touch a man with familiarity – a light touch on the shoulder – and I lay on my bed and cried. No one saw me. Prisoners, of course, suffer a loss of identity, but this light touch gave me a terrifying insight into the depth of my alienation.'

17 The Voice (III): A Nonce

The *Oxford English Dictionary* offers no definition of the word, and *Collins English Dictionary* defines it thinly as 'a rapist', which is only one segment of its meaning. There are tantalizing clues in 'nonage', meaning one's minority (the most typical application of the word nonce is to child sex offenders), and in 'nance' for homosexual. The current idea among prisoners was that the word derived from 'nonsense', but I found this unconvincing.

The nonces never talked about sex, except in a formal manner, because their sex was their hell. They are convicted of a different class of crime from everyone else, convicted and condemned not only in the eyes of the law but in the eyes of their fellow cons. One should not really say 'fellows' because nonces are no more regarded fraternally by other prisoners than are prison officers. In a riot, sex offenders are as much in danger as staff, and provide convenient hostages. They are, often literally, outcasts, frequently held in segregation for their own protection (at their own request or otherwise) under Rule 43 of the Prison Rules: 'Where it appears desirable, for the maintenance of good order or discipline or in his own interests, that a prisoner should not associate with other prisoners, either generally or for particular purposes, the governor may arrange for the prisoner's removal from association accordingly.' Another name for a nonce is a '43'.

He is not only an outcast but a scapegoat, whose presence is a source of constant complaint among other prisoners: complaints which pretend to spring from disgust but which are really the opportunity to assume moral superiority. Some other prisoners use the nonces to salve their own bruised consciences, drawing comfort from the belief that there is a class of deed by comparison with which your own looks almost good.

The crimes of Lewes's nonces cover the full range of nuance: heterosexual and homosexual rape, attempted rape, molestation of children and adults of both sexes, having sexual relations with minors, child murder following a sexual assault and abduction and sexual assault.

Benson's crime involved the last-mentioned.

Something about the way he carried himself told me he was a sex offender. His bearing made the shame that was in him visible. He was overweight, slow of movement and speech, and had a nasty nickname derived from his crime. Several cons told me privately how much he was disliked, and after a surprise altercation in a lifers' group meeting one morning, when he tried to have me excluded by raising an unsubstantiated objection to my presence (overruled by all the others), I could see why.

Only a few days before we had been talking amicably. Perhaps he had told me too much at once for him to bear.

'I was born in Swansea. My parents were a mixture of Scots and Welsh and my father was a butcher.

For the first ten years of my life, until he died, we lived very well: we had a good home, father had a decent income, and really we didn't want for anything. So the family background was quite good. The problem, really, was my mother. I disliked her as a person because she was, in my terms, rude, crude and very aggressive. The worst thing, and it's something I detest in people, was that when she was angry she started shouting; that was her all over.

She was a short, thick-set woman and very handy with her arm. Very strong arms. I was always at odds with the family, with the environment, things like that. But I think that what really soured the relationship between us was that I didn't like her and I wouldn't allow her to show me affection – I was conscious of these feelings although I couldn't put them into words.

Both my parents were long dead, thank God, by the time I first came into one of these places. This isn't my first sentence. The first time it happened I picked up a girl along with three Dutch guys who were all hitch-hiking by the side of the road. When the road split I let the Dutch guys out and we carried on.

We were driving for most of the day. In the evening I took her to dinner. We were talking and she told me about herself; she was about twenty-two, twenty-three. We were going along quite well and over dinner I made her a proposition: I would pay her £40 and she would have sex with me. She accepted and I gave her the money at the dinner table.

She knew the area and said she knew a spot, so we drove there and took the car into this field and stopped. But when we got there she reneged on the deal. I naturally remonstrated with her. I didn't want the money back: I was just very annoyed that she had conned me and that she wouldn't go through with it.

You see, I didn't want sex because of, well, because of sex. I was out to prove something to myself. I had become impotent and I wanted to find out if I could go through with it, and I was really annoyed that this girl had conned me. I was furious that after I had worked myself up to ask her and she had agreed and raised my expectations, she should now turn round and say no. So I hit her – just once, I slapped her across the face. She went for me and tried to strangle me, and in the course of that I pushed her out of the car on to the ground. I was going to drive away, but she was shouting: "Don't hit me, don't beat me!" I thought, hit you? I'll kick the living daylights out of you!

So I literally tore her clothes off and tied her to the door of the car and beat her with a dog collar. That attack was a very vicious attack. I hit her about thirty, forty times, very, very vicious, beating her on the genital area and on the back.

I tore up all her clothes so that she had none left. She had a bathing suit and that was it. After it was over I felt sorry for her and said, "Come on, I'll drive you into town and buy you a new dress"—at twelve o'clock at night! I just didn't know what was happening. I got ten years for that and served six.

At the moment I'm doing life for abduction, grievous bodily harm and sexual assault. The crime this time was against a twenty-eight-year-old American hitch-hiker. It happened in South Wales and it was more or less the same format as the other attack.

I met this girl and we spent the day together, touring round South Wales, and in the evening we had dinner. I was supposed to take her to meet some friends of hers but I couldn't find the place and in the course of searching I stopped the car. She was becoming very agitated and kept asking me, "Where are you going?" So I slapped her across the face. And that really precipitated the attack.

We drove around for another half-hour and then I suddenly turned off the road and drove into a field. I told the girl to get out of the car, which she did, and then I undressed her. I tied her up and hit her several times on various parts of her body with a piece of electric flex which had been in the boot of the car.

The attack itself lasted about five minutes, but then we spent almost twelve hours together, sitting in the car, just talking and things like that. She was very calm but obviously very confused and emotional because she couldn't understand me, and the transition from being a relatively nice guy to being horrible. She clearly didn't understand the reason for the attack and kept blaming herself. A lot of the time my role was reversed: I was trying to comfort her, to explain and reassure her that it really wasn't her fault. I had no intention of harming her further and I wanted to take her somewhere where she would feel safe and get treatment for the welts: to a hospital, to a police station, or even to try and find these friends of hers.

Eventually, at about seven the next morning, we ended up in a Roman Catholic church and I fell asleep on the pew. She had been sitting beside me and when I woke up there was this rather tall, dark-haired guy standing by me with another woman. He said this girl says you're bothering her and won't let her have her bags out of the car and we'd like you to leave her alone. So I gave her her bags, apologized and drove away.

I drove all over the place and ended up parked in a country lane somewhere, where I sat throughout the night in the car. There was a time early in the morning when I thought: well, you know, you're no good to anyone, you ought to end it all. So I got hold of a knife and slashed my arm. It was very deep, and eventually I thought, shit, I'd better do something about this. So I got a towel and cleaned it up. I thought the best thing you can do, boyo, is go and find the police.

I was glad that I never saw her again. It was bad enough to attack her without putting her through the trial as well. I pleaded guilty to all the charges, because I didn't want that girl to go through the trial. I just wouldn't do that.

At the same time, that's one of the worst aspects of it: you may be able to come to terms with yourself, to come to live with yourself, but you can never say you're sorry because there is no one to say sorry to. All right, it would be easy, I suppose, say, to write to the girl – I've thought of that and even written letters but never posted them. It's bad enough for her having memories of the attack, and no doubt her memories are as painful as the ones I say hurt me – and I never got attacked – without getting a letter out of the blue from this grotty little guy saying, "Oh, I'm so sorry, I didn't mean it, I had no intention of hurting you when I met you." That to me is obscene.

It's always rough for sex offenders in prison. You are the most disliked and lowest form of life in the place. You're going to be confronted physically sooner or later, and either you stand up for yourself or else you give way and become the stereotypical, cringing, pimple-faced sex fiend they see you as.

You're called a nonce because they say, "Oh, you've been up to nonsense." The most despised nonces are the child molesters, and then there's a sort of gradation from there upwards.

You're fixed with that image: that's it, and you are despised. It's very hurtful. Then of course they try and take it out on you physically. It was very unpleasant for me for the first eighteen months, when I was in the Scrubs – actually it was unpleasant before that, in the police cells where they kicked the shit out of me, holding me down and beating me in the same way I'd beaten the girl. They kept me stretched naked in a police cell for three days with the door open and an officer sitting in the doorway. They got a policewoman to come up and verbally abuse me. They kept waking me up in the middle of the night, accusing me of trying to commit suicide, or with a doctor who would wake me up and say, "Why did you do it? Why did you do it?" When I went to make a statement they said, "What happened?" I tried to tell them and they said, "Never mind all that, *this* is what happened." And then they dictated the statement.

With the cons I've had really bad sorts of experiences, starting with the Scrubs. Everyone knows what you're in for, they've been told, deliberately, by the screws. You get people walking by: "Ugh, nonce!" and spitting. Or else when you're playing football they act excessively rough, or they just come up and challenge you for anything at all at the first opportunity. You're living with fear all the time, every minute. For the first eighteen months I had a fight a week. Eventually I got left alone, but you can never become part of the con street.

Also, I found, because I am quite well educated, that that set me apart. It's a "bad thing" in prison, because it makes the others feel insecure. They'll use you. I mean I used to have people ask me to write letters for them or write their petitions; then they turn round and say, "Oh you think you're so fucking clever."

The worst thing about it all is that you're never allowed to forget your crime and never allowed to escape the feelings you have about it. You might be in a queue for something or other, and you hear someone referring to "a nonce". Whether it's you or not, immediately your ears prick up. Or it might just be a throwaway comment: someone passing in the corridor will say to his mate, "Fucking nonces, I hate them." They have this self-righteousness about them. You've given them that.

In the cinemas here, inevitably, they have pretty sexy films. All these guys will be sitting there saying, "Oh lovely! Get 'em off!" and all this sort of thing. All of them sit there absolutely enthralled watching an attack on a woman, and then afterwards you'll hear someone say, "Yeah, all these fucking nonces, they love doing that kind of thing, don't they." And they're quite serious.

They have to have these very sharp divisions between people, and they have to put you in this category or that one after they know what your crime is. If you are a nonce, then, true enough, you are forever one. And the worst part of it is, they try to elevate themselves at your expense. If you're the sort who won't take it, then they don't know how to handle that and their response is violent. And the violence they use, or are prepared to use, is probably greater than the violence I've ever used, if we're talking about the actual mechanics of an attack.

The most common acccusation I get is that I've committed my crimes because I like doing them – because, you know, that's the way I get my kicks. But I ask, who's getting the real kicks? My case got a centre-page spread in the Sunday newspapers, thousands of extra copies were printed, *and* they exaggerate it for delight of their readers. And the worst element is that, all the way through, no one asks you why. Oh, they'll ask, "Why did you do this?" But all they're looking for is an explanation which will make sense in their own terms.'

18 'Valley To The Captain'

Mrs Ina Baker was surprised, but not displeased, when the small bespectacled man stopped her in the Station Road, Bexhill, and said:

'I know you.'

He seemed to have made a mistake. Mrs Baker had to look more closely to be sure. Then she said in a friendly voice:

'No you don't.'

She was about to pass on without another word when the man said:

'Well, I knew your husband.'

Mrs Baker stopped as she heard the words and looked at the man again. She was eighty-seven and her husband had died four years ago. The little man must have had something to do with the youth club which Mr Baker ran at the Methodist church for over twenty years. She asked the man if this was so, but instead of answering her he said, looking out from behind his thick glasses and smiling:

'I've always admired your husband.'

These were pleasant words to hear. Mrs Baker acknowledged the compliment with a smile and a grateful nod of her head. The man went on:

'I belong to the Methodist Church too. I'm on my way to the chemist just now – I suffer terribly from headaches, you see – but if you like I'll stop by and have a cup of tea with you later.'

Mrs Baker was happy to have met an admirer of her husband – and just like that, by accident! She agreed to the man's suggestion and, after telling him where she lived, went home to put the kettle on. Ten minutes later he knocked on the door and came in.

He was in his mid-sixties, with grey hair swept back from his forehead, and was well-spoken. They drank tea and talked in a general way about Mr Baker (as the man respectfully called him) and about the man himself. He was a Scotsman and his name was Andrew Stuart.

'That's a good Scottish name,' said Mrs Baker.

He worked on the cruise liner, QE II, as a valet to the captain.

Mrs Baker was very impressed. She liked men in uniform, and admired her new friend all the more for the information he had just given her, even though he was in ordinary clothes – she supposed he would call them 'civvies' – at the moment. Her admiration was soon mixed with pity, however, when Mr Stuart – he asked her to call him Andrew, but she didn't like to yet – told her that he was unmarried, indeed that he was an 'orphan', without any family. 'Orphan' sounded strange coming from a man of pensionable age, but somehow that made it seem all the more sad to her.

After they had talked for a long time about lots of different things, he suddenly offered to give her his name 'in writing', and the telephone number of the place where he stayed when he was in Southampton. Mrs Baker thought it was a nice suggestion. She handed him a slip of paper from the writing pad on the bureau and he used his own Biro pen to write:

Andrew Stuart, Valley to the Captain, *Queen Elizabeth II*

Underneath he added a Southampton address and telephone number. Mrs Baker took the piece of paper from him and read what was written on it. She was unable to prevent herself from pointing out that he had misspelt the word for his job. Andrew looked out at her from behind the thick lenses and said:

'Oh, did I?'

But he didn't offer to change it.

After that, they fell into another conversation and before either of them was aware of it it was getting dark outside. Mrs Baker closed the curtains. Andrew was worried about getting back from Bexhill to Southampton at such an hour. Mrs Baker thought he would have no difficulty catching a train at this time. It was only ten o'clock. She was about to offer her bed-settee to him anyway but before she had a chance to do so, Andrew asked. Just for one night, he said. She said of course he could.

In the morning it was nice to have someone to cook breakfast for.

They started chatting again and Andrew stayed for lunch and then tea, and although she was a little surprised when, come evening and darkness, he once again made no move to leave, Mrs Baker had no deep objection to making up the bed-settee for him a second night.

While she smoothed out the sheets and placed the blankets on top and tucked in the sides, Andrew kept on talking. He talked a lot about his work. Mrs Baker didn't mind that. She was interested to hear about life on board the famous liner. He asked her if she had ever thought of taking a cruise, and she laughed and said she was getting too old to think about that sort of thing. But she liked the idea of it.

Andrew also mentioned that he had meant to buy a new coat of a kind essential to his work, but that he had forgotten to bring his chequebook with him from Southampton. He had seen the very coat he wanted in a shop in Bexhill. It was 'choice', he said, as if he had been talking about meats. It cost £200.

'If by any chance you could lend me the money,' he said, 'I'd pay you two hundred and fifty pounds back.'

Mrs Baker was startled by the suggestion that she might require interest on a loan. It struck her as coarse and she hadn't thought of Andrew like that. She quickly assured him that she would have no need of an extra £50 on her money when it was returned.

'I've no money in the house,' she told him. 'But in the morning I'll go to the bank and get it for you.'

Then they went their separate ways to bed and in the morning, after she had cooked another large breakfast of bacon and sausage and egg – his favourite, he said – he accompanied her to Barclays Bank.

On the way, Andrew asked:

'Can you lend me a thousand pounds?'

'As well as the two hundred pounds?'

'I'm very well paid, you see. A thousand pounds a month. Great money on the QE II – if only I could get at it. You see, the purser himself is taking care of my satchel for me, and he's in. . . .'

No further explanation was needed for Mrs Baker. She didn't like talking about money. Andrew's face spoke for him. He was well-mannered and well-dressed. All the clothes he was wearing were in line with that £200 coat he needed to buy. So, at the bank, Mrs Baker spoke to one of the personal managers and arranged a £1,190 overdraft on the spot. She then wrote out two cheques for the money, cashed them and gave the money to Andrew.

'I'll get my purser to send you the money,' he said on their way out of the bank. 'A cheque for twelve hundred and fifty pounds – made out to you.'

He was smiling broadly. Once again she was a little annoyed by the suggestion of something extra. But she didn't say anything about it and they talked of other things as she walked with him to Bexhill railway station. As he boarded the train, he reassured her once more about the loan.

Funny, she thought when he had gone, he didn't buy the coat after all.

Miss Mary Simpson went for a cruise on the liner *Canberra* and had the time of her life.

That was three years ago. So when she was in a café in the centre of Worthing having morning coffee and a scone, and overheard the man and woman at the next table talking about the very same thing, she leaned closer to them to try and hear what they were saying about it.

Her hearing was perfectly good, but since the accident her sight hadn't been the same – she was eighty-six – and by a funny linking motion which she was aware of but unable to do anything about, she tended to lean closer to people when they spoke to her as if she needed them to speak up, whereas in fact she really just wanted to see them better. Anyway, she was rather hoping to join in this conversation and tell the pair that she had been on the ship. He was saying that he worked on it.

After about a minute of waiting, she was given her opportunity. The woman, seeing she was taking an interest in what they were saying, glanced up at her and smiled. Miss Simpson said:

'Oh, sorry to interrupt. But I've been on the *Canberra*, you know.'

The grey-haired man with the Scottish accent eagerly told her that it was his job to look after the captain – 'Valet to the captain,' he said, smiling with pride, 'that's me!'

Miss Simpson asked him where the *Canberra* was now and he told her that it was docked in Southampton and would not be moving until just before Christmas. Miss Simpson thought it was odd that a sea-going man should refer to his ship as 'it', especially the lovely *Canberra*. He asked her if she had ever thought of taking another cruise. She replied that she would love to but didn't think she could afford to spend that amount of money on a winter holiday.

The captain's valet smiled and turned around a little more in his seat, the better to face her. He said he would be able to procure a £200 discount for her. If she was prepared to give him £200 down he would see about all the arrangements as soon as possible. In the meantime she should give him her name and address so that he could send her the brochure for the Christmas cruise.

It was 20 November, and Mary Simpson thought that that was possibly a little late to begin making arrangements for a cruise at Christmas time; but then she had no other plans and she had enjoyed the last one very much. She gave the man her name and address on a piece of paper which he produced, and he said he would send her the details. Then she thanked him and left to catch the bus home, feeling quite excited.

When the door-bell rang early next morning while she was eating breakfast she thought it must be the postman with one of the catalogues she had sent away for or else a man to inspect the gas meter.

She opened the door.

'It's me,' a small figure said cheerily.

At these moments her sight seemed to get worse, embarrassing her.

'Who?'

'Andrew.'

'Andrew?' Then, as she said the name, she remembered. She had recognized the accent without being able to place it. 'Oh yes. You'd better come in.'

She poured him a cup of tea from the pot which was still warm. He was on his way to Southampton, he said, but didn't have to be there until the next day. He would be looking for a place to stay the night – anything would do for him, even a bed-settee.

Miss Simpson supposed he was thinking of going to a guest house.

'You won't have any trouble,' she said.

Over tea they chatted about the *Canberra* cruise again and she said: 'While you're here, why don't I write you a cheque for two hundred pounds?'

Andrew seemed about to say something and then to stop himself.

'That would be fine,' he said at last. 'If you want to give it to me now you can. But cash.'

Miss Simpson said she would have to go to the bank, in that case, and Andrew said why didn't they go now. He could come with her and leave his bag here.

They went on the bus. He paid her fare, which didn't cost much, though she considered it gentlemanly of him to do so. On the way he talked more about his work and said there were some things he needed to buy here in Worthing, things for his work. The only trouble was he had gone and forgotten his chequebook. Left it in Southampton.

If she could lend him some now he would make sure it was returned to her as soon as he got back to his ship. How much? Oh, about a thousand.

This meant going to the building society first and then the bank. She drew £500 out of one and £750 from the other. Then she gave both lots to Andrew. He thanked her. Now he would be able to buy the things he needed, he said.

She had remarked how well dressed he was when she first met him. It was one of the things she noticed about people in spite of her eyesight. He told her that a captain's valet had to be very smart about his appearance. Take this coat he was wearing, for example. On its own it cost £200.

After coffee in a place she recommended in Church Street, they returned

to Miss Simpson's flat where Andrew picked up his bag. He said he would
be getting an earlier train than he had first thought, and that he wouldn't
be needing a place to stay after all.

She heard what he said but didn't really think about it properly until
afterwards. He left to catch the 12.30 train.

Andrew had had a bad run on the horses. Every day he bought the *Sporting
Life* and he always bet with Mecca. He had first learned the word from a
book as a child, and he said it brought him luck. Mecca.

Lucky wasn't quite the right word to describe him. He wasn't lucky, he
was skilful. He knew the horses. He had won thousands of pounds on the
horses in his time. Always the horses, never the dogs or the casino.

Thousands of pounds. But not now. In two months he had lost all the
money borrowed from Ina Baker and Mary Simpson, plus a bigger loan of
almost £2,500 from Doris Gwyn, with whom he had stayed for three
weeks. She had wanted him to look after her (she was seventy-nine) but he
couldn't stay. He had done a lot for her in those three weeks, including
getting a good deal for her on a brand new colour television set.

He had been well off and living high but now he was broke again.
However, he could congratulate himself on having been sufficiently fore-
sighted to pay his landlady in Eastbourne a month's rent in advance at the
end of last week.

Mrs Fowler was a very nice lady. Her guest house was a family sort of
place. You ate with them and watched television with them. Andrew liked
that and told the family how much he appreciated their family ways. He
was an orphan, he said.

He told them all about the QE II and how he would be setting off on it
again the month after next. He knew they liked hearing about his work
because they asked him lots of questions.

One evening the family and a few guests, including Andrew, were
watching television in the front room after a nice meal cooked by Mrs
Fowler. *Crimewatch* came on, the programme which asks for public help in
tracking down criminals who are active in the area. Andrew was hardly
watching it. The programme held no interest for him. It was always the
same. Have-you-seen-this-man? He never had.

He was sitting in his armchair, half-looking at the *Daily Telegraph*, on
the brink of dozing off, when the presenter mentioned a con-man who had
been working in the south coast area. Andrew glanced up and found his
own face looking back at him from the television screen.

He recognized the photograph instantly: it had been snapped on one of those cameras which gives instant photographs by a woman in Oxford who had lent him £1,000. He was very well dressed in it.

'. . . anyone who has seen or thinks they have seen this man is asked to contact. . . .'

'Andrew.' Mrs Fowler looked round. 'That's you, isn't it?'

There was something which touched him in her voice. It wasn't angry, just surprised. He was conscious of everyone in the room looking at him. The programme had already switched to another feature, about someone who pretended to be an inspector of gas meters.

'That's you, Andrew,' Mrs Fowler said again.

'Is it?' He leaned forward in his chair as though his picture was still on the screen. The false meter man, he heard the man in the programme say, might be violent. Andrew hated that. He had never been violent.

'I'll have to go and make a phone call, Andrew,' Mrs Fowler said rising from her chair. There was a little more anger in her voice now and Andrew felt betrayed by that more than what she intended doing.

'No, wait a minute—'

Andrew followed her into the hall. Mr Fowler followed him, without saying anything. Andrew tried to think of something to say to Mrs Fowler, while Mr Fowler stood in the open doorway with his arms at his sides, but nothing would come out.

When the door-bell rang, Mr Fowler answered it. It was the police. Mrs Fowler's daughter, who lived in a house two streets away and was in Mrs Fowler's house every day, had seen the programme too.

Andrew got the job in the officers' tea-room opposite my cell after Richard failed to return from court just before Christmas. It was a good job and Andrew was fully aware of its benefits.

He made a good cup of tea. I savoured it myself, but he made a point of telling me anyway.

'They all say I make a much better cup of tea than the last bloke who was in here.'

He also regarded himself as a model prisoner, and told me that as well.

'If they left that gate open I wouldn't walk out of it,' he said with finality, as if giving conclusive proof of his fitness of character.

He was eager to tell me of his exploits. He was proud of his skill at conning people (he had no aversion to the phrase, although he hated to be called a thief: people gave him their money willingly, he said) and was disappointed to be back in prison. Just under a year ago he had been released on parole, after serving two years out of a three-year sentence for deception.

Now he was awaiting further sentence having pleaded guilty to the charges involving Mrs Baker, Miss Simpson and Mrs Gwyn. Before beginning that sentence – it would doubtless be more severe than the last – he would have to make up his broken parole and serve the remainder of his previous sentence. He was sixty-three now, and unlikely to be out of prison again before he was seventy. His wife had left him and the little business he had had was in ruins.

Nevertheless, he intended making a new start once he was released and to break his habit of seeking easy money.

'I'll have to,' he said, 'now that they've had me on that programme.'

The whole sorry outcome he blamed on the authorities' failure to provide properly for him following his release on parole. They had sent him to a hostel which not only contained a lot of ex-convicts who were bad company and a bad influence, but which had a reputation guaranteed to frighten prospective employers to whom Andrew went looking for a job. As much, if not more, than the prison authorities, he blamed the BBC for 'ruining' him.

'My name's mud now,' he said, shaking his head indignantly.

Andrew was fastidious about prisons and the type of people you were forced to associate with in them, and was clearly pleased to have come across someone he thought was 'decent', whom he regarded as a social equal, or even – more gratifying to him, for sure – as a superior.

After our first conversation in the tea-room he regularly knocked on my door, morning and afternoon, with a tray bearing a mug of tea and a plate of biscuits. Whenever I saw that face appear round the door I couldn't help thinking that I was being made to play captain to his valet. The idea of accepting payment from me for this refreshment, according to the arrangement in the tea-room, embarrassed him deeply, and he took my money only because I insisted, placing it in the tin box with reluctance.

I asked how many 'loans' he had received during his career. Roughly forty, he said. He had never been refused.

'Everybody says I've got an open, honest face, and I'm always well dressed and well-mannered; and if you're well brought up and put on the airs and graces, then you can't fail. At least, I can't. I've got the knack, you see.

'And I always ask for a thousand. None of this five or ten or twenty business, like some people. Never less than a thousand for me, please. These people, you see, they handed me their money. They trusted me. I only had to ask. One old lady in Morecambe gave me two and a half thousand pounds and never reported it.' He smiled, thinking of the kindness. 'I never beat them up or anything like that.' He made a recoiling gesture with his hands, showing that the very suggestion revolted him. 'Or raped them or burgled their houses. I couldn't do that sort of thing. They all said how kind I was and what a pleasant person I had seemed. You see, I'm always nicely turned out.'

He touched his well-pressed prison shirt with his fingertips, as if smoothing the lapels of a £200 coat.

19 The Case Of Colin Wallace

They are all obsessed by their cases. A large proportion – perhaps a fifth – claim to be innocent and some have grown to believe it.

The prisoner protesting his innocence does not automatically gain the sympathy of the others. Some are ridiculed. Others talk about it perpetually and never converse. If they do ask a question, it is only as a stepping-stone, a pause before the next instalment of the story. Or to telling the same instalment again.

Down in the block, Kerr had spent the past eighteen months, some of it on 'hunger strike' he said, as part of his campaign to prove himself innocent of the murder of an old man, for which he received life imprisonment.

He looked at me hesitantly. 'You need a champion.'

He brought out newspaper clippings, depositions, retractions by witnesses at the trial, letters from supporters . . . and he managed, somehow, to undermine at every step any confidence one might have had in him.

'You need a champion,' he said again, looking at me aslant. Then: 'That Ludovic Kennedy – I'd love to get in touch with him. Here, you don't have his address, do you?'

I didn't, but said that he could probably write to him, like any member of the public, care of the television company he worked for.

'Could I?'

'What's to stop you?'

Some days later, I was chatting to someone who had just completed a spell in the block.

'Old Kerr tells me you're getting Ludovic Kennedy to have a look at his case.'

Ben Brown was different. He was a tall, sad-eyed, childlike man in middle age, of deep feeling and intelligence. As a juvenile he had killed a member of his own family and served a life term, getting released in 1954. Since then he had kept out of trouble, though he had spent short periods in mental hospitals. Fourteen months before I met him, convinced that the woman he was living with was 'up to something' with the man next door, he smashed the windows of his own house. The police were called and it was discovered that Ben was a lifer. His licence was revoked, he was recalled to prison, and now had no immediate prospect of release. He talked about nothing else.

Others – Bulletproof Joe was one – claimed to be not guilty of the specific charges laid against them, without denying a long history of crime. Joe was angry and almost driven mad by his frustration, but others accepted that such are the rules of a game of chance.

There were two men, with no previous records, who said they were innocent of the crimes they were convicted of. Both gave good reason for believing in them.

One was Miller Steele, the young New Zealander jailed on a charge of drug smuggling. He served just over half of his two-year sentence and was released on parole in the spring of 1985. The other was a more complex case by far; and it involved a more complex man.

John Colin Wallace[1] was a Senior Information Officer in the British Army, serving in Northern Ireland in the army's Information Policy Unit in the early 1970s. The Unit was in effect a black propaganda and psychological warfare agency attached to the press desk at Army Headquarters in Co. Antrim. In 1980 Wallace described his job to an Irish journalist as the spreading of 'what he called black propaganda and misinformation aimed at discrediting various individuals or groups'; mainly, of course, individuals associated with the IRA or comparable paramilitary organizations. An example of these 'black propaganda' tactics involved inventing a story about IRA members using dogs for target practice, after a number of canine corpses were discovered in Belfast. In fact, according to the magazine *Time Out*, the dogs had been killed by British night patrol soldiers who feared that the dogs might give them away.

Another story was put out in 1974 after Merlyn Rees, then Northern Ireland Secretary, arranged a ceasefire with the IRA and began releasing internees. This was resented by army officers. An army spokesman blamed recent violence on the policy and produced figures which suggested that over half of those released had become involved with violence again within a few weeks, whereas the true figure was less than 20 per cent.

The Government, dissatisfied with the way the army had been handling press relations – which it felt had often worked against its own policies and interests in the province – instigated a major shake-up of the information services. One

[1] Colin Wallace offered to allow his real name to be used in this account and after some consideration I accepted. So much has appeared in the press about the case – and is likely to continue to appear – that it seems pointless to pretend to be talking about someone else.

result was Wallace's departure from the army and Belfast in 1975, the official reason being that he gave a restricted document to a journalist.

He himself cites another reason. At the time he had been trying, in vain, to bring to light a long history of sexual offences committed against boys at the Kincora Boys' Home in Belfast and had come to believe that the scandal was being suppressed for political reasons. Leading figures in the political world of Belfast were involved. Wallace was the author of a confidential report, commissioned by the Information Policy Unit in 1974 to examine links between homosexuals and the paramilitary group, Tara. His report indicated that such links did exist and that homosexual abuse of boys had been taking place for many years, yet no action followed. Wallace claims to have been disgusted and disillusioned by this lack of response.

Then, in 1981, William McGrath, the leader of Tara, and two others were prosecuted for a string of offences involving boys at the Home — offences to which Wallace, in his report, had alerted Government intelligence as early as 1974. The report was published in the *Irish Times* of 26 June 1985, with the deletion of many names. Wallace concluded:

> I am far from happy with the quality of the information on this matter, and I am even more unhappy because of the, as yet unexplained, failure of the RUC or the NIO [Northern Ireland Office] to take on this task.
>
> I find it very difficult to accept that the RUC consistently failed to take action on such serious allegations unless they had received some form of policy direction. Such direction could only have come from a very high political or police level. If that is the case then we should be even more wary about getting involved.

The affair involved not only the offences for which McGrath and others were prosecuted, but tales of witchcraft and the murder of a young boy. Wallace's report substantiates his claim that a cover-up took place, and its very existence appears to contradict the findings of a 1982 enquiry, which reported that there was no knowledge of this affair on the part of the military authorities.

After leaving the army Colin Wallace moved to England, settling with his wife in the town of Arundel, Sussex. He took a job as Information Officer for Arun Council, while his wife worked as secretary to the local nobility. In the summer of 1980 he was charged with murdering the husband of his assistant at the Council, with whom he had been having an affair. Following a trial at Lewes Crown Court, he was convicted on a reduced charge of manslaughter and sentenced to ten years' imprisonment.

He was the first prisoner I spoke to in the prison. On an early visit after talking to the Governor, I was taken on a tour of the prison by officer Hull. He arranged a brief meeting with the two orderlies in the education department. Colin worked as a secretary, doing typing, filing, paperwork, etc, while his assistant, William, kept the place clean and made endless cups of tea and coffee.

A more strongly contrasting pair could not be imagined. Whereas William (who was serving life for child murder) was introverted to the point of stammering incoherence, Colin was confident and forthright, remarkably fluent, cheerful and intelligent. He was of medium height, well-built, bald, with metal-framed glasses, and aged about forty.

It was a warm August day and we sat in one of the classrooms drinking coffee. Colin wore the regulation sky-blue T-shirt and I noticed how milky-white this first prisoner's arms were. On that occasion he smiled and joked a good deal, at once surprising and reassuring me, sketching out a rough picture of life in prison and contrasting it with the view the public had. When I left I said I looked forward to seeing him and William again. I couldn't say precisely when I would be returning.

'We'll be here anyway,' he said.

In the summer of 1980 Arun district was selected by the BBC to take part in its television game *It's a Knockout*, and Colin Wallace was appointed to act as link-man between the Council and the television team. While preparations for the show were being made, he began the affair – sexual but never fully consummated – with his assistant at the Council office, a younger married woman called Jane Lewis. She and her husband Jonathan were friends of the Wallaces and the two couples often met socially, but Colin and Jane had succeeded in keeping their relationship secret from their respective spouses. Mrs Wallace suspected nothing, but Jonathan had become suspicious.

On the evening of 5 August, when filming for the *It's a Knockout* heat was completed, a celebratory dinner was to be held for the participants and helpers in the Avisford Hotel in Arundel. The Wallaces and the Lewises were both invited, naturally, and a special presentation of a photograph was to be made by Colin to Jane in appreciation of her good work in helping to organize the event. The two women met early in the evening to play squash. Without their knowledge, their husbands had also arranged to meet.

Up to this point the facts are verifiable. What happened afterwards is heavily, and critically, in dispute. One man died and another was imprisoned for it – wrongly, he says.

Colin Wallace maintains that he picked up Jonathan Lewis in his car in

Arundel at 6.30 p.m. and drove back with him to the Wallaces' house in Dalloway Road. There they had one drink each – beer for Colin, gin and tonic for Jonathan – while talking about various matters, including the somewhat troubled state of the Lewises' marriage, without involving, according to Colin, any detailed discussion of the clandestine liaison between him and Jane, although at one point Jonathan asked, hesitantly, if they were having an affair. Colin denied that they were.

At about 7.15 he drove Jonathan into the centre of Arundel, leaving him, at the latter's own request, at Surridge's newsagent's shop, where he gave the impression he had arranged to meet someone else. Colin claims that this is the last time he saw Jonathan Lewis. He then returned home, washed and quickly changed, and set out for the hotel where the dinner was being held, expecting Jonathan to arrive – a 'little late' according to what he had said – within an hour.

Halfway through the dinner, at 10.15, Colin began to suffer from serious stomach pains of a sort which had frequently troubled him lately. A few nights before, the Wallaces had had to cancel an engagement because of the complaint. He left the hotel and drove to his home to get some medicine, before returning to take his place at the table again.

That is Colin's story. The police reconstruction of that three-quarters of an hour, and their interpretation of certain events later – the version presented by the prosecution at the trial – is very different. In this version, Jonathan arrived at Colin's house and accepted a drink. A discussion began about Colin's relationship with Jane, developing into an argument, during which Colin felled Jonathan with a single blow to the face, hitting him between nose and upper lip with the heel off his hand, causing a hairline fracture of the skull and knocking him unconscious. Then, believing him to be dead, Colin carried Jonathan outside and bundled him into the boot of the *It's a Knockout* car which was parked in the drive. There he left him while he washed, changed his clothes, set to rights any trace of a struggle, and afterwards proceeded to the Avisford Hotel. Three hours later, at 10.15, he excused himself and left the table on the pretext of suffering from a severely upset stomach, made a brief and presumably desperate tour of the area in the car in search of a suitable place to dump the victim, finally choosing Gasworks Lane. There, in full view of a busy bridge which crosses the River Arun in the very centre of the town, he disposed of Jonathan, still breathing but unconscious.

Witnesses reported that he returned to the hotel dining room after his twenty-minute absence sweating heavily but otherwise lacking the signs of a struggle or any of the unease which might be expected in a man who had just committed the murder of a close friend.

Jonathan's body was not found for three days. During that time Colin was questioned but not initially considered a suspect. He did not mention to police that he had seen Jonathan between 6.30 and 7.15 on the night of his disappearance.

When Jonathan's body was finally dragged out of the River Arun, police at first stated that foul play was not suspected. He had a fractured skull but the actual cause of death was drowning, as shown by the amount of water in the lungs. His fly was undone and the tip of his penis was sticking out over the top of his underpants. It was surmised that he had slipped while urinating into the river, struck his head on a rock, lost consciousness or somehow got into difficulty, and drowned.

Before long, however, the police were making further investigations. In Jonathan's diary they found an entry for Tuesday 5 August: 'Colin 6.30'. The Chief Constable of Sussex Police Force had by now declared himself satisfied that it was a case of murder. When members of the force next interviewed Colin Wallace, he denied having seen Jonathan at the time they suggested. Upon entering the dining room at the Avisford Hotel on the night in question he had remarked that Jonathan was going to be late, citing as the source of this knowledge a telephone call in mid-afternoon. So when, confronted by the diary, he finally admitted to having seen Jonathan at the time they suggested, the police naturally asked why he was so eager to keep this 6.30 meeting secret.

Colin was snagged. The police suggested that the afternoon telephone call had never taken place, although Jane, who was present at the time, confirmed that it did. Colin claims that since his wife did not know about the 6.30 meeting – arranged, after all, to discuss certain matters concerning Jane Lewis of which she was ignorant – to have refrained from mentioning it at the time of the dinner was, under the circumstances, quite normal. To have brought it up later on when worries about Jonathan were beginning to arise but not yet to spread, would have blown his cover and, again, raised suspicions in his wife's mind that Jonathan, Jane and Colin knew something which she did not. Having embarked on that course, having offered that story, he was bound to stick to it if he did not wish to threaten his marriage anymore than it already was threatened. He decided, very foolishly as it turned out, to give the same story to the police.

Not a single item of hard evidence exists to support the charge that Colin Wallace killed Jonathan Lewis. In his summing up, the judge remarked that all of it was circumstantial. There were no hairs, no traces of a struggle in the car, on the accused (for example, bruising or grazing) or in his living room; most surprisingly, there was no blood which could definitely be traced to the deceased, no fingerprints and no fibres to match those of a man who was supposed to have lain for three and a half hours in the boot of the car, in an unconscious or semiconscious state, while his attacker dined a few yards away and plotted how to get rid of him finally.

On the other hand, the sheer amount of circumstantial evidence lends force, if only at first glance, to the allegation. There is the failure to inform anyone, and the later denial, that he had seen Jonathan earlier in the evening. There is the absence from the dinner table. And there is the evidence of witnesses who saw Colin cleaning out the boot of the car at 5.30 the following morning outside the offices of Arun Council. Pinpricks of blood were discovered in the boot of the car but British Leyland workers appeared at the trial to testify that on the day when this particular vehicle was constructed, they had reported injuries to hands. There is considerable dispute about whether the tiny spots could have come from someone of Jonathan's blood group, but the actual location of the spots suggests that the blood was spattered during the construction of the car.

Colin explains his absence during the dinner by saying that he had to return home to fetch some medicine for an upset stomach; both Mrs Wallace and Mrs Lewis acknowledge that he suffered from such a complaint. As for cleaning the boot of the car, this had to be done, he says, prior to the *It's a Knockout* car being returned to British Leyland that morning, as arranged.

Along with his wife and others, Colin had been up all night helping to comfort Mrs Lewis, and felt he might as well make an early start on what was an obligatory task. When the contents of the boot were recovered, no blood or suspicious traces were found on them, nor on the cloth which was used in the cleaning. Moreover, he says that if he had been set on destroying the evidence of a murder, he would not have chosen his own office car park as the place to do it.

One of the first people Jane Lewis telephoned from her house while her fears for Jonathan increased was a business associate of his, who was referred to at the trial as 'Mr Y'. Some weeks before, Jonathan had told his wife of certain difficulties he was experiencing with business associates and said to her that if anything ever happened to him she should 'look out for Mr Y'. A friend of the Lewises who was present in the house through the early morning of 6 August, John Muggeridge, told how in the weeks before his disappearance Jonathan had been reluctant to drive his own car – a conspicuous orange Volvo – and had often asked Mr Muggeridge to ferry him in his car. His fear may have had something to do with the fact that he was owed a substantial sum of money by Mr Y.

At about 1.30 a.m. Jane Lewis telephoned Mrs Y – from whom Mr Y was separated, though they remained in close contact – and asked if she knew of any appointment which involved their respective husbands that evening. Mrs Y replied that to her knowledge the two men had planned to dine with some American customers. Early next morning John Muggeridge asked Mr Y about the appointment. He replied that the customers were his and that Jonathan had not been involved. When police later asked Mr Y to account for his movements, he said that he had been at his girlfriend's address all evening.

There is no suggestion that Mr Y had anything to do with the death of Jonathan, but it seems to be one of several matters which have not been satisfactorily cleared up.

And there are other matters which, according to Colin and his solicitors, have not been fully investigated. He has set these out in successive letters to the Secretary of State at the Home Office in an effort, so far a vain one, to have his case reopened.

For example, at midnight on 5 August an independent witness – a fisherman called Hart – saw a figure searching the riverbed with a torch at the point at which Jonathan is supposed to have entered the river. Who was this person and what was he doing? Despite appeals he has never come forward. Moreover, as Colin has written, 'If as the police submit, Jonathan was dumped into the river at the mouth of the sluice gate at approximately 10.30 p.m., there would have been insufficient water in the river at that point to carry away the body until the next high tide. [A note at this point refers readers to 'data provided by the Southern Water Authority'.] If that is the case then the mysterious stranger seen by Mr Hart could not possibly have failed to see the body – he was seen searching that exact spot by torchlight.' On the night Jonathan died he took his briefcase with him when he left home; £200 in cash was in his pocket when he was found in the river. This would indicate that he was expecting to do some business that evening after seeing Colin but before the dinner party. To put it another way, why should he take a large sum of money, plus briefcase, to a party where he was not expected to pay for anything? His watch was found at a spot fifty yards south of the place where he supposedly entered the river, while his keys were found to the north. This contradicts the suggestion that the unconscious body was dumped straight out of the car. On the night before his death he was seen in the Arundel swimming pool car park – where, for a reason not yet explained, he had taken to parking his car while riding in other people's – with a woman (not his wife) who has not been identified.

What's more, Jonathan was over six foot tall, whereas Colin is five-ten and a stone lighter. It was a summer's evening, dinner time. The Wallaces live in a suburban street. The task of bundling the unconscious body of a bigger, heavier man into the boot of a car would be a difficult one, though it is feasible. It is, equally, plausible that the victim would remain unconscious in the boot – if not, why didn't he leave fingerprints and make a noise? – for three and a half hours, and that his alleged attacker could be sure he would do so while he dined in polite company (including a police superintendent) a short distance away. It is possible, though scarcely imaginable.

The mystery deepens yet further, bringing attention back to Colin Wallace's military background. Some time before Jonathan Lewis's death Colin received a telephone call from a press agency in London. The caller said they had been given his name by a contact in the Ministry of Defence. They were producing 'some type of promotional material' dealing with the sale of a particular type of parachute which could be used in either civilian sports or in a military role. The contact had informed them, correctly, that Colin possessed such a parachute. The caller also knew, presumably from the same source, that Colin had spent a brief spell with the New Zealand Army SAS. Would he be willing to pose for photographs taken of him with the parachute in both civilian and military roles? Colin assented, although there was no fee involved. He contacted a local freelance photographer, who took the pictures. When the shots had been taken, Colin rang the agency, who then asked if four-foot enlargements could be made. Colin put this request to the photographer, who said the task would be impossible for him. Then, when Colin tried to get back to the agency to explain the photographer's problem, he found the number unobtainable. Directory enquiries said that that number did not exist and was not listed under the name of Kaymar Studios, the name the agency had given. The photographer produced contact sheets and a bill, which he gave to Colin, but because of the apparent, unexpected termination of the request – Colin had no address to which to send them, and knows only that the agency was based 'somewhere on the southern outskirts of London' – nothing further was done.

Although somewhat puzzled, Colin forgot about Kaymar Studios, until the photograph of him in military gear, sporting New Zealand Army SAS insignia on his beret, turned up in court as support for the prosecution's allegation that he had been trained in karate while in the army, and was therefore capable of delivering the blow which, it is supposed, stunned Jonathan Lewis. How the prosecution came by the photographs is a mystery. Colin denies ever having had such training; the Ministry of Defence refuses to confirm or deny if that is the case.

There is also the tale of how the army tried to pin on him a charge of possessing a stolen firearm, and another of missing files in the MOD, in RUC headquarters and in Arun Council.

All this took place before anything happened to Jonathan Lewis, and neither Colin nor any member of his camp has been able to do more than point to certain coincidences and say that it appears that someone – with what intention no one can definitely say – had been keeping an eye on the man who tried to make public a scandal in Northern Ireland which, in the words of his original report, 'a very high political or police level' wished to keep quiet.

Nor did Colin cease his efforts to have Kincora investigated after his imprisonment. In the year he went to jail, 1981, William McGrath was successfully prosecuted for offences committed at the Home. Then, in 1982, following persistent rumours of a cover-up, the British Government ordered an investigation to report on whether these allegations had any substance. The enquiry, which said there was no evidence of knowledge on the part of the military authorities – knowledge which the publication of Senior Information Officer Wallace's document now proves they did have – was carried out by Sussex Police Force, which had recently completed its prosecution of Colin Wallace.

All agree that there was no hard evidence to convict Colin Wallace. On the other hand, one's instinct leads one to protest, if he had nothing whatever to do with the crime then surely there would be at least a shred of proof on his side to support his claims. After all, it is possible that, while the prosecution's reconstruction of the killing is inaccurate in certain particulars, he carried out the deed in an altogether different way.

One thing could have cleared it up for the accused and ruled him out of police enquiries: a credible witness who saw Jonathan alive after Colin claims he dropped him off at the newsagent's shop in the centre of Arundel at 7.15 p.m. Such a sighting would confirm that Jonathan was still alive while Colin was comfortably ensconsed at the Avisford Hotel. There is such a witness. She came forward after public appeals before Colin's arrest, and appeared at the trial.

Amanda Metcalfe worked in the bar of her parents' hotel, The Golden Goose, on the eastern outskirts of Arundel. Her normal working practice was to serve in the bar until 7 p.m. Tuesday was her usual night off. On 5 August, however, she was forced to break both of these habits, since there was a change in the routine of the bar staff. A different barman from usual began at seven o'clock and Miss Metcalfe stayed in the bar to assist him. While he served, she collected empty glasses.

During one of her rounds of the tables, she caught sight of a man she had seen in the bar on several previous occasions. She did not know his name but usually he came in with a woman she took to be his wife. Tonight Jonathan Lewis was dressed more smartly than usual in a beige suit and tie, and he was accompanied by another man.

At the trial Miss Metcalfe was asked if the man Jonathan was with in the bar after 7 p.m. was Colin Wallace. She said that she could not be sure, but added: 'He had more hair than he [Wallace] had.' She also believed the other man to be older. The judge and jury accepted her version of events in all but one crucial detail: they decided she must have confused her dates.

Colin Wallace now claims to have the evidence to support Miss Metcalf's assertion that 5 August was indeed the date when she saw Jonathan in the bar of her parents' hotel while Colin was in company elsewhere. When Mrs Lewis returned from the dinner party she checked through her husband's wardrobe in order to deduce what clothes he had been wearing, so that a description could be given to the police. She found dry-cleaning labels and a crumpled polythene covering which had been removed from the suit that evening before Jonathan put it on to go out, first to Colin's house and then the dinner party. It is generally agreed that Jonathan was seldom in the habit of wearing a suit, collar and tie, and it now appears that he could not have worn this outfit on the previous evening to that on which he died, since the suit was probably at the dry cleaner's. It should be remembered that Amanda Metcalfe made her claim to have seen the dead man only days after his disappearance was announced.

Colin was obsessed with his case. In almost every conversation I had with him the subject was raised within five minutes or less, sometimes without preamble, so that he would begin talking about it, as it were, in the middle of a sentence. I estimate that we spoke for a total of about thirty hours; not once during that time did he drop his guard, contradict himself, or give the appearance of having to think hard to maintain consistency. And I heard no stories from other prisoners of him having done so.

He had compiled dossiers of forensic, medical and factual evidence which conflicted with that offered by the prosecution at his trial, and he seemed to be always awaiting a reply to his latest missive to the Secretary of State at the Home Office, who repeatedly declared himself 'satisfied that these matters were fully and properly investigated'.

My own feelings about the case were and remain a tangle. The prosecution case, as I studied it, only confused them further. Whoever killed Jonathan Lewis, it was surely not done in the alleged way. A Harley Street pathologist engaged by the defence in 1981, Professor Keith Mant, concluded in his report based on examination of the injuries to the body and the place where it was supposed to have entered the river: 'It would appear that the reconstruction of events by the police is wrong if Mr Wallace is involved.' Had Colin spotted this misconstruction as the loophole to his own eventual pardon?

Finally, I had to admit that the case was intellectually inscrutable. Trying to penetrate it was like attempting to answer the question of God's existence: every argument in favour produced a counter-argument against, and in the end one was thrown back on faith.

The force of one's belief in Colin inevitably met another, equally strong force, emerging from a knowledge of his work in Northern Ireland. He was, as the press dubbed him at the trial, the master of black propaganda. I found I experienced the same sort of feeling as I'd had during visits to East European countries, where tales of bugging and spying, even among those one had taken to be friends, are so widespread, and the suspicion created by them so pervasive, that finally one cannot even rely on the evidence of one's senses. This or that seems plausible, even verifiable – but then your perception may be just another part of the illusion.

Colin knew that he had helped to prepare the gallows he stood upon. When he first raised the matter of the Boys' Home scandal to an Irish journalist, in the early 1970s, the journalist was unwilling to accept *this* item as genuine, knowing that so many others emanating from the Information Officer's desk were false.

I myself believed in Colin's innocence, but knew that no one could be certain, finally, that he did not kill Jonathan Lewis. Except Colin himself? What does Colin know? In 1980, the year of his arrest, he told the same journalist (cited by Liz Curtis in *Ireland: the Propaganda War*, Pluto Press, 1984):

If you are in the Int world – especially army intelligence, you are in a totally unreal world. You are always at war, even in peace-time. You don't exist, you have no legal standing. You see conspiracies everywhere. Ordinary rules don't apply. . . .

20 Kum By Yah

The only time I'd opened a Bible was when I was serving time in Lewes prison. That was a really hard nick and you did every moment of your sentence. They never paid you enough to buy both snout and papers, so I used to tear a page out of the Bible and roll in that. It was nice thin paper and made a good smoke. Trouble was, the screws were wise to this particular trick and they'd check the Bible once a week. I've done bread and water for using it for smokes — so far as I was concerned the Bible offered no consolations!

Ken Lancaster, *The Love Hammer*

'If you want to see us as we really are,' a young lifer suggested, 'as we are in ourselves, you should come to a church service.'

The Roman Catholic Mass, which he attended, was given every Saturday morning, and the Church of England service was held on Sundays. Worshippers of both denominations congregated in the small, modern chapel to the north of A Wing, between the wing and the sports pitches. In the prison there were also Methodists, Moslems, Sikhs, a Buddhist, and members of other religions and sects; most received attention in their cells or at regular intervals in a suitable meeting place.

The prison Chaplain is Church of England; the Roman Catholic priest comes in to give Mass on Saturdays, and then for special events and dispensations. Next door to my room on B Wing, the Chaplain had his rooms: an office and adjoining meeting room, converted out of three former cells.

When the prison was completed in 1853, the Chaplain occupied one of the two projections which flank the main gate — now in use as the Governor's offices — while the Governor resided in the other. Today's Chaplain lives more modestly in a terraced house on the main road, only yards from the prison walls.

It goes almost without saying that if you are waiting to be saved, prison is as good a place as any to let it happen. It had happened to Kenny, the ventriloquist, to the son-of-the-chief, and to others. It had happened, many years ago, to Ken Lancaster, author of *The Love Hammer*.

He 'heard a voice' one night in his cell, he wrote, after refusing to attend church. One evening he came to preach to a gathering of cons at a chaplaincy meeting, but the message – which was essentially that if he could be saved, anyone could – was never delivered, as first one prisoner and then another mounted his hobby horse and took advantage of the audience to scatter personal grievances at large.

For some men, religion seemed to be a poetic approach to private loss, a means of lyricizing pain. For others it was a revelation of a life with places for charity, mercy and love. For yet others it offered a possible link to parole – many had a policy of missing no chances – or just a way out of the wing on a Sunday morning. And there were some who tried, without succeeding, to anchor themselves to a faith.

How important is the prison chaplain? I would say that as a symbol within the scheme of punishment, he is next in importance only to the governor. He represents the mirror-image of the governor, who, irrespective of the injustice of such a view, inevitably appears as a barrier to freedom, whereas the chaplain stands as a beacon to it. It is the aspiration of the chaplain to guide the man to a grander conception of the idea of freedom than the open gate represents. He is, or ought to be, an inexhaustible source of consolation in a punitive universe. Like a good singer, a good prison chaplain should be capable of inspiring dull lines to profundity.

The Reverend Ball is a tall, lean man, with dark hair and a fresh complexion. Spectacles suggest a scholarly bent in an otherwise boyish character. Sometimes, in accordance with his duties, he could be seen moving around the wing in ecclesiastical garb, while at other times, though he was never without the dog collar, he wore a sports jacket and denim jeans. Wrapped around his waist if he was in church dress, or attached to his trouser belt when in civvies, was the chain bearing his pass key.

Tony Ball has been a priest for sixteen years, has been in prison service for four, and been at Lewes since October 1983.

'When I was at theological college we had contact with two local borstals, and quite by accident I got involved with the boys from the borstals, and I began to think that that was the sort of work I was being called to do. I didn't give it any more serious thought, however, until the end of 1981, when I had done six years' work with my parish and had realized that the time had come to move on. I looked again at the prison service and thought that this would be a good time to see if I could do the work, if I was *meant* to do it, in that sense.

'Liverpool was a good introduction to the prison service – a large prison, numerically about two and half times as large as this, a big, rambling old place. I remember being impressed by the size of it when I walked in at first

— the wings seemed to be miles high and miles long — and also by the noise. I had a picture in my mind that it'd be almost like a hospital, you know, that hushed silence — in fact, there were a lot of people moving around, a lot of doors banging and clanging. I was an absolute novice as far as the chaplaincy was concerned, though I was an experienced priest. The mistake I made at first was of trying not to remind prisoners that they were prisoners; trying to talk, for example, about the slop-out as "emptying your potty in the bathroom". You soon get that knocked out of you.'

His duties cover basically the same ground as those of any of his colleagues who work in parishes around the country: discussing matters of faith and what it means to be a Christian, meanwhile fulfilling the ministerial role in bereavement, prison deaths, the occasional wedding, and also conducting services in the prison chapel.

The Reverend Ball was an optimist. The morning after the chaplaincy meeting at which Ken Lancaster had been prevented from speaking, he came into my room and told me that he felt bad about it having been a failure. No discussion had got started and no one left with a sense of discovery. One man walked out in the middle, and at least one other had badly wanted to. But it achieved something none the less, he felt, in giving some of the fellows a chance to air their grievances. (I had to admit that I thought they had been airing these same grievances day-in and day-out for years and that the previous night's exercise made no difference.)

Rev. Ball disliked calling the prisoners 'inmates', preferring 'fellahs' and one of his greatest pleasures stemmed from the letters he received from ex- cons who took the trouble to write to him, a reminder, as he put it, 'of their bad old days'. Perhaps by the very nature of his conspicuous role in the world of the Good, a clergyman will be regarded with suspicion by those whom the law has consigned to the domain of the Bad; a prison chaplain's effort in overleaping this suspicion must be greater than that of most others; he is supposed to reach out the hand of mercy — but, like that of the unmerciful, his hand holds a key.

'Keys are seen by inmates as being a sign that you are a part of the establishment. You have a cell key, you have a pass key . . . therefore, you're not one of us, you're one of them. My own way of trying to get round that is by saying that keys have a twofold purpose: a key will lock a door or a key will open a door; and I don't need a key to lock any cell door in this prison, but I do need a key to open up the door and reach a man.'

The main purpose of his ministry, he said, was exactly as it would be in a parish: to bring Christ into this place. A pragmatist as well as an optimist, he was prepared to measure his success relatively.

'When I came here, I found C Wing particularly difficult. We had three inmates – three fellahs – out of about 150 who actually came to church. My first impression when I went on the wing was that I was a sheet of glass: people just looked through me. I felt miserable about it, and it took weeks and months to get over it. Now I feel that I've got a good relationship with the majority of them – though it's inevitable that there will be some who are not well-disposed – and although I'm not into playing the numbers game, I get tremendous satisfaction from seeing the increase in the number attending chapel: and not just chapel but Bible-study groups and all the other things that the chaplaincy puts on. I get satisfaction from it not only because it's my job, but because it reaches back to my reasons for joining the prison service. I felt that the Church outside, and perhaps a good percentage of the community, would see criminals as of little worth. I just couldn't accept that. One of the basic Christian beliefs, for me, is that it is in every man to change, and that every man, irrespective of what other people think of him – good, bad, indifferent – is still a child of God. I really do believe that.'

I turned up for the Church of England service at 8.45 a.m. on a wet Sunday morning, joining the few others who had come in from outside, in the waiting room which adjoins the main gate.

There were four of them: two elderly ladies and two men, one of them in his late forties and the other about the same age as the women. There was something about their behaviour, with each other and with me, which struck me as abnormal and limited to this specific type of community: the same bland advertising of the 'good news' which has put me off church congregations all my life.

The Chaplain collected us and we filed along behind him in the rain to the chapel.

The view from the chapel is splendid: sloping downs fold upon one another in varied shades of green. There are no bars on the windows – the only windows in the prison without them – but brackets attached to the wall on the outside prevent the windows opening any more than a few inches. The frames are formed of small metal squares which it would be impossible to slip through.

I tried to seclude myself at the end of a pew, but one of the ladies adopted me. She asked who I was and why I was in the prison, then introduced me (by my first name) to the others (by their surnames). She drew me into the middle of the pew beside her and talked about the prisoners she visited. Did I know this one or that one? Then she riffled through her handbag and emerged with one of these stapled booklets which evangelists hand out on street corners. It was called 'The Voice'. It contained statements from ex-prisoners who had been saved by the Word. There was a photograph of each one, smiling, mostly pictured in living rooms with their families.

One of the men tapped me on the shoulder from behind and asked if by any chance I could play the organ. The usual organist was ill and hadn't turned up. I answered that I could not, and so we spiritedly prepared ourselves to sing the hymns unaccompanied.

Wing by wing, the prisoners filed in: F Wing first, then C Wing, then the hospital and finally the Segregation Unit, whose solitary detainees cannot be denied worship. (The young offenders have their own service.) The prisoners' entry was greeted with enthusiasm by the four visitors, and accompanied by a great deal of handshaking. It seemed wrong, somehow, that we visitors should have misappropriated the proper duties of the hosts. My friend met an African prisoner as he came through the door. He seemed pleased to see her. I discovered later that she was his regular, and only, visitor, since he, like many Africans in Lewes, had come straight to the prison from Gatwick Airport – the only two parts of England he had seen and ever would see.

The Chaplain opened the service with a prayer. Then we sang, first 'Amazing Grace' – the most popular song – followed by another spiritual, 'Kum by yah'. During these and other, more orthodox hymns, the only voices which one could actually say were *singing* came from the Africans, who sat apart from the others on their own pew.

There were five of them, including the man who had been talking to the old lady at the beginning. They flung their heads to the ceiling and abandoned themselves to the song, using hands and arms and even their torsos to express themselves, as they sang loudly, not caring for discordance or disharmony, unaware of the timidity which restrained the rest of us.

> Kum by yah, Lord, kum by yah.
> Kum by yah, Lord, kum by yah.
> Kum by yah, Lord, kum by yah.
>
> Someone's singing, Lord, kum by yah.
> Someone's singing, Lord, kum by yah.
> Someone's singing, Lord, kum by yah.
> Oh Lord, kum by yah.
>
> Someone's sleeping, Lord, Kum by yah ... .

I listened for their high-headed worship every time the singing started, regretting the shamefulness of my own, but glad, after all, that the organist had not come.

Then came the lesson. The son-of-the-chief stepped forward from the front row to read it, from Genesis, Chapter II:

> Therefore is the name of it called Babel; because the Lord did there confound the language of the earth; and from thence did the Lord scatter them abroad upon the face of the earth.

At the back of the chapel, by the door, which was kept locked, three prison officers were on duty, dressed in full uniform. One was wearing an overcoat, because of the rain outside, and kept his cap on his head throughout. Strapped to his chest, under the coat, was a walkie-talkie radio. If anything suspicious or dangerous happened in church, assistance would be at the doors within seconds.

But the only disturbance was the constant giggling of a group of cons whom I recognized from C Wing as self-appointed hard men. Their repressed laughter interrupted prayers and the petitions offered on behalf of friends and families. It would not have been proper for the officer to intervene here, and in any case he offered his own disruption, keeping the volume of his walkie-talkie up high, so that messages buzzed intrusively through the chapel at all points in the service: during the lesson, the sermon, the prayers and the hymns.

We sang again, after communion had been given to the ring of kneeling prisoners, and again the voice of the Africans soared triumphantly above the rest, mercifully drowning out the electronic babble coming from inside the officer's coat. I thought that if Christ could come into this place, as the Chaplain wished him to, it would be through the expression of their unmelodious, discordant cry.

Finally, we lowered our heads and the Chaplain began to intone:

'The Lord be with you.'

And, as we, the people, replied, 'And also with you', another, disembodied, staccato commanded:

'*Officer Parker to report to A Wing office please, over* . . .'

'The peace of God, which passes all understanding, keep your hearts and minds in the knowledge and love of God . . .'

'*Senior Officer Jenkins to see the Chief in his office, over* . . .'

'And the blessing of God almighty, the Father, the Son and the Holy Spirit, be among you and remain . . .'

'*Officer Blakey wanted at* AG's *office right away.* . . .'

21 Secrets

Secrecy is an essential part of the apparatus of confinement. The exterior of the prison is shrouded in secrecy – if nothing else, the wall maintains it: the state's effort to conceal its chaos from the people. And the secrets which the system keeps from its captives means it holds the power of imbalance over them. For these secrets inevitably concern what the system regards as the prisoner's *real self*.

The prisoner's natural condition is paranoid; he sees his life as being governed by secrets others hold about him. In an extreme form, this leads to imagining that there is another him, existing only on paper, in forms – the Governor's memo and the Home Office file – and that it is on this version of him that judgements will be based and decisions taken. The actual him, the one moving from landing to landing and cell to cell, is irrelevant; he exists merely to be the victim of whatever measures are taken against his paper self.

The only privacy one can have in this state is another secret. For the prisoner, secrets are part of a hunt for privacy, which to the confined man is an emblem of freedom.

Some prisoners wanted to suggest that they possessed information which it would be in my interests to obtain. One man came every day for a fortnight, saying that if I meant to tell 'the truth' about this place, then what he knew was essential to my story. What was it? He wouldn't say. There was no overt suggestion of bargaining – his secret was evidently too precious for that – and I found out nothing more. It would have been surprising to discover that there was anything to disclose.

My presence contradicted the principle of secrecy, and from the first I had a role thrust on me of secret-gatherer. My status being anomalous, prisoners saw an opportunity to entrust me with information they found too burdensome, or to show a private self which they feared the authorities or their fellow cons could not appreciate.

Augustus

He asked me to call him that, the little grey-haired man. He was about sixty. When he arrived at Gatwick Airport on a business trip from his native country, his suitcase was examined and found to have a false bottom with a large quantity of cocaine stored underneath. The customs officers were less surprised, he said, than he himself was, and he proceeded to tell me in detail how he had been tricked and coerced into carrying the load.

A plausible story, like so many.

At the end of his tale, Augustus smiled wearily and began to talk about his family. He has at least another three years of this doubly alien life to endure before being released for deportation. And what then?

More than anyone else, he looked out of place, walking along the landing from cell to toilet like a frail child who by accident has landed in the toughest class in school. One evening I watched him playing table-tennis. He patted the ball back across the table to his opponent, listlessly, without flair or motivation, to a huge defeat.

He had about him an air of gentility in its most admirable form. He seemed well-bred. Prison had debased and humbled him, but his good manners, his attribution of worth to his interlocutor, were, one felt, a more durable part than that which had been permanently changed by the shock of prison.

One evening he came to my room and, after we had spoken for half an hour, pledged me to secrecy on a matter which, if it became widely known, could be fatal for him: *he was a former policeman.*

Then he left the room, relieved, unburdened, infused with a sense of having been intimate with another human being at last – the first time in a five-year sentence.

Trustie

'Trusties' are trusted prisoners – trusted, that is, not by the cons but the staff. They are often empowered to work outside, in the gardens, or in the officers' mess. Trusties are usually short-term prisoners, or else ones who are nearing the end of a sentence, for whom escape is pointless.

Someone told me never to trust a trusted prisoner – a motto which matched my instinct – and it was clear that staff trusted them no more than anyone else, but simply used them. A trustie often has some other line: he may be a grass, or a money lender; or else he simply wants to be seen to be on the side of the Good.

Wood told me, 'I'm a trusted prisoner.' It was the first thing he said. Then he asked if I wanted to have a note of his number and cell. Unable to think why I might need them, I said no.

Wood proceeded to tell a long story about his criminal past and how his life had been changed when he met the girl with whom and with whose parents he had been living at the time of his arrest. The parents were 'quite well off', he said.

Although he had intended to go on seeing the girl, he had decided one day to move out of their house. On that day something else happened: the house was burgled.

Wood was arrested, and to his embarrassment his criminal past came to the notice of his girl and her parents for the first time. He was sentenced to two years' imprisonment – on a charge of burgling the house of the girl he loved.

I realized that he saw me as an official. That was why he wanted to give me his prison number. Thinking I was a keeper of records and files, he hoped I might do something for him. I had formed no firm opinion of whether his story was true or not, but I found that I was unable to take much interest in it. Perhaps his introductory 'I'm a trusted prisoner' had clouded my view of him. As he worked in the officers' mess I hardly ever saw him, and eventually forgot him.

Some time later he appeared at my door with hand outstretched.

'I'm leaving,' he said.

'Oh? When?'

'In quarter of an hour.'

Someone else had, unexpectedly, confessed to the crime for which he was imprisoned and signed a statement. Wood was being released on bail pending further investigation of the claim. I said goodbye and watched him walk back down the corridor in the direction of the Assistant Governor – an accomplice now, in securing his release, rather than an opponent – who was conferring with another officer on this or some other matter.

Three hours later I happened to see Wood walking into the probation officer's room.

'Haven't you gone yet?' I asked. His face was set firm and his mind was elsewhere. He didn't hear me.

Someone standing nearby told me that when Wood got down to the gate, having said goodbye to all his old cronies, been wished good luck from every quarter, passed through Reception and changed into his own clothes, signed whatever forms they asked him to sign, picked up his property — after doing all this he crossed the threshold to the free world only to feel a hand clamp his shoulder: an old, familiar clamp.

'Two gentlemen to see you,' somebody muttered. The girlfriend, who accepted every word of Wood's story, was standing there. He hadn't even had a chance to embrace her.

The policemen wanted to talk about an unpaid fine of several hundred pounds, dating back some years. Wood's memory of the event was vague but, he had to admit, unshakeable. Naturally, he didn't have the money on him, and neither did the girl. The police would not accept her cheque.

So back Wood went, a victim of gate arrest, through Reception, where he put on his old gear, up to the wing, where he had to bear the mixed pity and laughter of those he had left behind only half an hour before.

Born again

For weeks I thought his name was Paddy. People called him that, even screws, and he answered to it. When he showed me a letter beginning 'Dear Terence', I asked him how it came to be. He simply shrugged and pointed to the letter, saying, 'That's my name: Terence.'

His new name, he should have said. Inside, they still called him Paddy.

Paddy had been a habitual, petty criminal since he was a child in Belfast. His father, a drunk, had beat him regularly and beat his mother, and Paddy recalled how he first stole a bicycle because of, not despite, the threat that if he did wrong he would be taken away from his mum and dad.

Now in his early twenties, he had spent at least a quarter of his life in penal institutions. Yet he was eager and cheerful, athletic and incorrigibly hearty. The crude tattoos which decorated arms, hands, neck and forehead contrasted strangely with this pleasant boyishness.

But Paddy had a reason for joy. The letter he held so proudly to show me came from a member of the church he had joined six months earlier. He had never met the sender, but that made him all the more thankful to have received the letter. This person, he pointed out, was not the first from the church who had cared enough about him to write. All his flashy friends on the out had come up to see him once, maybe twice, and then fallen away. 'But these people just keep coming up. They showed me that there *is* another life.'

Paddy kept a Bible in his cell, which he read nightly, though it meant taking a bit of stick from his mates. Occasionally he would quote to me from scripture, or recommend a book written by a Christian, and more than once came to my room to ask my opinion on a matter of some importance.

When the Ethiopian Jews were airlifted to Israel, to the world's surprise, Paddy was elated.

'Great news, isn't it?'

I said I wasn't sure.

'Why not? They'll have food there, sure.'

'But they'll be stepping, in a single day, from the environment which shaped their traditions to one which may resent them.'

'Nonsense! Israel's a religious country.'

Another time he asked what I thought about the theory, which he was currently studying, that God was an astronaut.

Not much, I said.

'I'm not so quick about it as you,' Paddy scolded. Then he pondered, fingering the tattoo of a spider's web on his neck. 'How would *you* explain it? The Holy Ghost.'

I mumbled darkly about a mystery, which caused Paddy to shake his head impatiently. He was fast losing faith in me. The new world he was set to enter should at least have the virtue over the old of certainty.

At about that time he began to have his tattoos removed. One by one – first hands, then neck, then the forehead – they plucked the old icons from his skin: the spider's web; LOVE/HATE; a sword enwrapped with jewels; and a crude skull and crossbones from his forehead.

Curiously, in my eyes, their removal made him seem older not younger, more scarred and worn than before. I had grown to accept Paddy's decorations as part of Paddy; without them he looked like someone after amputation. But he was glad to see them go. They were, he complained, reminders of a criminal past – of burglary, kyting, false friends and false gold – which he had renounced for good.

In six months he was due for release and for the first time in his life he knew what was right and wrong. He had stopped swearing. He had stopped thinking ill of others and started looking for the good in them. Most important, he had discovered a force in himself.

'I've always had a heart but I've never used it. Now I can, and I want to try and help people – people like them in here – because I've got something to tell them, if they'll listen, even though I'm only a babe in this new world myself.'

The wedding

Michael was serving life for murder – or manslaughter, or attempted murder, or robbery with violence. I never found out, because each time Michael talked about it he told a different story.

In some ways there was no nicer, politer person in the place. He was forever courteous, friendly, welcoming, ready with a joke or a tease, particularly about this or that female teacher, though never crudely. He was also perceptive about many things, readily passing on his street wisdom, gained in Brixton, especially on matters pertaining to women.

This was incongruous as Michael had been inside (on this sentence) since the age of seventeen. He was now twenty-five. That meant not only that his experience was likely to be limited, but also that he had had plenty of time in which to forget whatever it had taught him. There is not much opportunity for practice in prison. Yet his instinct for the behaviour, the needs and desires, of the opposite sex always impressed me.

On the other side of this attractive aspect of his personality was a touch-paper readiness to react with violence. Michael boasted of being the victor in many fights, fights with prison officers, fights I suspected he had never had. And he boasted also of fights he was going to have when he was released, as well as the grand feats he was going to achieve.

'When you out there, man, you have to prove you can *be* somebody.'

Michael's father was Cuban; his mother was English. They kept in close touch, visiting him regularly, sending letters, making sure he 'wanted for nothing'. Michael boasted that they were very rich. I was unsure how seriously to take this claim – a lot of prisoners seemed to have rich connections – but one day, as if intuiting my doubt, he brought in a batch of photographs and showed them to me one by one.

'This here's my Mum; this is Dad; and this is my little brother.'

I saw a slim, handsome woman, a rather overweight man, beaming proudly, and a young man with a similar complexion to Michael. They looked happy, untouched by disaster.

'This isn't the brother who was killed in the Falklands, is it?'

'No, that was my other brother. These were all taken at our place.'

The atmosphere and the setting were merely suggested, since the photographs were all taken at night and out of doors; but if this was a garden, then it was part of a splendid house. There was a patio, an outdoor dance floor, a swimming pool and much else to hint at the spectacular residence to which they were attached. I admired all the photographs, asking questions about each in turn, then handed them back to him.

As he was leaving, Michael said he had just 'given it' to a screw. I acted unsurprised.

'Why?'

'Got fed up with him asking me stupid questions.'

'Like what?'

'Like: "How come you got a white mother?" Every time I see this screw he asks the same fucking thing. He was on visits once when my people came up and since then he's been asking, "How come you got a white mother?" So I give it to him.'

About a week later, he turned up with some news.

'I'm getting married.'

'Congratulations.'

Michael laughed. 'I mean it.'

'Who to? When?'

'You remember them photographs? Right. Well, remember the chick standing with my brother – that one.'

There had been another group of photographs besides those which showed his parents. In some there were young girls dancing, or cavorting frivolously before the camera. I remembered a young black girl standing apart from his brother, though in the same group, and assumed he must mean her. But just then he brought out the pictures again and shuffled through them until he reached the one he wanted: not the one I had in mind but another; in it his brother was shown embracing a blonde.

'That's her. Lucy. Little pet, she is.'

I preferred the other. Lucy had blonde hair and looks, but nothing to rely upon. Besides she was kissing his brother.

Michael sensed my unease.

'I told my baby brother: look after her. So he takes her along to parties and that, so she don't miss out. They've known each other since school, she and my brother has. Real old pals.' Michael smiled at the image. 'He's all right, my brother.'

Apparently the girl had been urging him to accept her proposal for some time, but only the day before, when she had come on a visit with his mother, had he finally accepted. Still, he wanted to quiet some doubts.

'As an older person,' he asked, turning serious, 'what would you say was the best thing to do in the circumstances?'

I asked why he was doing it: was it to help hasten his release? If so, it was understandable – most people in prison would do anything to get out – but he should be aware of it. I also wanted to know how long this girl had been waiting and how long she was prepared to wait. If it wasn't an impertinent question, why was a twenty-four-year-old blonde so desperate to marry a lifer? A man, furthermore, whom she had had little opportunity of seeing over the last eight years. Michael answered the questions at length. There were no two ways about it. 'She's after my blood, man.' But he still hadn't made up his mind, he wanted to think more about it, and he was glad to have had the benefit of 'an older person's' advice.

'Don't mention it,' I said, and he was gone.

For about two weeks after that it was the wedding, the wedding, nothing but the wedding. Then it was dropped and never another word was heard about it. I didn't bring it up because Michael was in danger of being a bore on the subject, but he acted now – speaking in his old sharky, fancy-free way – as if there had never been the hint of a wedding: no Lucy and no mother pushing him towards it, no brother playing the chaperone until Michael came home to take his rightful place as her husband.

22 Muscles

Skintalk

The professional tattoo is one of the souvenirs of a well-travelled man. While someone else might keep the overlapping labels of shipping companies and hotels plastered on his suitcase, the tattooist carries these labels on himself. Often the design enshrines a loved one's name, as if to pledge fidelity in faraway places, or else it takes the shape of an exotic bird, a snake or a dragon. The word is of Polynesian origin, *tatau* or *tatu* (though the practice is ancient), and presumably attained common usage in English through the experience of sailors who dabbled in tribal customs.

The prison tattoo brands a separate tribe. Prison jobs are easily distinguishable from the professional sort. They are usually asymmetrical, badly placed and ill-designed. They can be done in a number of ways; most commonly by a needle with thread wound round the point which is dipped in ink. The needle then punctures the skin, leaving its pigment underneath; this process is repeated, stab after tiny stab, until the design is made, a process which can last through many painful hours.

Almost any part of the body is game for ornamentation: forehead, cheeks, nose, neck, ears, back, buttocks, shoulders, thighs, feet, even the foreskin. . . . For the man on the out, tattoos proclaim a colourful past; for man-in-prison they are there to do something similar, only more urgently: to enhance the character which is otherwise in danger of disappearing into neutrality. They distinguish *this* body from a mass of bodies.

Claude Lévi-Strauss explained the skin-painting of a tribe of Central American Indians as 'the phantasm of a society ardently and insatiably seeking a means of expressing symbolically the institutions it might have. . . .'

So: here we have women's names, skulls and crossbones, swastikas, knives, genitalia, a crucifix, a question mark. They make statements, espouse beliefs, record friendships, provide a plan of action. They can also make the body into a wall upon which to scrawl graffiti: across one prisoner's shoulder was printed the message – 'The woman I love most was fucked every night by another man: my mother.'

It might be possible for an assiduous researcher to calculate how many terms a man had served just by scrutinizing his tattoos and differentiating inks and designs, and it was not uncommon for prisoners who had achieved an inner resolution to disassociate themselves from these 'institutions', symbolically expressed, by asking to have their tattoos removed while they were inside.

'That young man's made good progress since we've had him,' an Assistant Governor says during a chat at the wing office. 'When he came in here a year ago his whole face was covered in tattoos.'

The prisoner, his neck still a babble of words and signs, pads past, aware he is being talked about. A mute greeting is forced from his bleached face.

A visit

Since yesterday or the day before he has shown signs of getting ready – having a haircut, keeping aside a clean set of clothes – but really he has been preparing for this visit since the last one, a month ago.

Who is going on the visit? Not this one, not N24138, not this caricature in prison gear – no, a free man, a man with a wife. This morning N24138 had to go to work as usual: a reminder that he is a man without manliness, a shadow, a ward, a slip of the mind. But this afternoon – from one-thirty until three-thirty, to be precise – a man! A family man!

For most prisoners, visits are the sole temporary escape from the punishment. The cubicles, in which the two parties are separated by wire or glass, still remain, but for the majority visits take place in a room which resembles a cheap café.

What does he expect from the visit? He always hopes it will bring something he does not quite know the shape of, and therefore cannot name; something possibly stretching back to first love. Usually, though not always, he is disappointed, recognizing well before the time is up that he is bored. Perhaps it is in the nature of conversations begun in that cramped, busy, smoky room that they will dry up in the speakers' mouths before achieving a satisfying end. The screws – though she has told him that they are polite when she arrives and departs and when they are groping in her handbag – sit near the door looking fed up, until calling time at the end, like in a pub.

Yet his anticipation never quails. Here, once a month, he flexes an old set of muscles. He knows her every movement on the day, from putting on her make-up before the mirror in the morning to arriving at the station in town. The train gets in an hour early, she is always at the gate on the dot.

Sometimes they take a quarter of an hour to call him. He hates that, even though they run out of things to say before the end. But the worst part comes when she has booked in, had her papers checked, her handbag searched, and been sent to wait in the corridor adjacent to the visiting room. Then the officer hands the visiting order to another officer who gives it to another. This one comes to the door of the workshop and makes a public broadcast:

'D—, you've got a visit!'

Then the rub-down, and sometimes a look accompanying it: 'Who the hell would want to visit *you*?'; and the suspicion that someone deep inside himself, another voice, shares this disbelief. And finally there is the message, conveyed by her worried look when she first sees him where he hoped to find a smile, that while this is release for him it is punishment for her.

One more! One more!

Exercise may be taken in the yard – 'if weather permits', according to the rules – or else in the gym. In the yard it is exercise in name only for all but a few. Some jog round the sports pitch; groups of two and three stroll in a circle; others are content just to sit or stand and peer at the sky. Officers look on silently with arms folded, walkie-talkies strapped to their chests; then a signal is given and the group is shepherded back inside.

In the gym it is different. It is the most popular place in the prison. Physical training is the body's hour of revenge for the slanders of the system against it.

Some display themselves ostentatiously, while others work privately, silently, in a corner: lean keep-fit fanatics, fatsos dreaming of turning it into muscle, spluttering weightlifters – 'one more! one more!' – dancing badminton players, self flogging hyperactive self, big ones with limbs swollen to tree trunks, little ones with tree-trunk biceps but calves like twigs, tacticians plotting survival, beauty queens preening themselves for evening parade.

It occurred to me that the amount of force in this small room, if quantified and sent for trial by a jury charged with measuring its potential for violence, would draw a very long sentence. Nor does the paradox of the system equipping men with superb bodies, which would serve them well in the event of a riot, go unremarked by prison staff.

But for the moment all physical activity is ordered and structured, shaped by play, the aesthetics of the match, and dedication to an ancient ideal. Or you could see it like kitten's fun, a harmless version of the defensive and aggressive strategies required in later life.

The lesson

The education block is light. The department is situated on one floor of a building constructed with the help of prisoners in the late 1970s. It is reached by way of a short corridor attached to B Wing. Prisoners on their way to classes assembled at the gate outside the door of my room and were led through the corridor and upstairs to the department by an officer who remained on duty there throughout the morning, afternoon and evening sessions.

Under the Education Officer and his Deputy work three full-time teachers, plus a part-time staff of about eighteen. The Governor and two education officers had between them developed a programme which included maths, English, drama, history and current affairs, French, Spanish and social skills; there were also facilities for arts and crafts, pottery and guitar classes, and a variety of computer and video equipment. A handful of prisoners were studying for the Open University while others would be sitting O-levels.

There are five classrooms and the department can accommodate up to fifty pupils at a time. To qualify for enrolment, C Wing residents need only enquire about available places and then begin attending at the start of the next session. However, the prison climate, the prison culture, is not kind to a spirit of enquiry or the sort of improvement envisaged by the education department. In spite of the efforts of education staff and the genial, relatively free air of the department, staffed by a strongly-motivated workforce, most classes were under-subscribed. Just over a fifth of convicted men attended classes at the time of asking.

The education department was one of the things the Governor was most eager to show me when I first arrived; he was rightly proud of it and assumed, again rightly, that I would be able to relax in the reduced pressure of its lighter spaces.

'On one level', he said, 'the prison has to continue to be run efficiently.

Now, you can if you want to – and a lot of governors do – run the place according to the rule book. But there is a more imaginative way of interpreting the rules, to encourage personal growth within the rigid prison system. If you're not careful, men can go through their sentences with their deepest problems untouched. We aim to offer some kind of aid to those people with problems.'

He was referring to problems of alcohol, gambling and drug addiction; emotional, sexual and mental problems. In particular, the education department can address itself to illiteracy and lack of social skills – not to mention the problems which emerge from a feeling that life is static, the body inactive and time dead.

A man of thirty cannot read or write; another cannot speak English; another is a kleptomaniac; another, serving ten years, has just heard from his wife that she no longer intends to visit him; another has no wife and no relatives or friends anyway but is about to be released after sixteen years; another apologizes for having been 'in here so long I can't think straight any more'; another fears the giddying prospect of release more than the familiar fact of confinement; another will be met at the gate by his heroin addiction; another tried to castrate himself with a razor blade; another disputes his conviction on a charge of rape on the grounds that all his life he's been impotent; another grapples with homosexuality today as he did with celibacy yesterday; another lives in constant fear of attack from other prisoners; another is going to a psychiatric prison where 'they break your personality down into little pieces and then start building it up again'. . . .

Besides the education department, a network of services – chief among them the welfare and medical services and the chaplaincy – operates within the prison to attend to prisoners' problems. But, like all prisons of its kind, Lewes has scant resources to devote to healing – whether by orthodox methods or by other, perhaps more imaginative efforts. Here, as everywhere, the main emphasis must be on security. The rule book may be interpreted imaginatively, but its austere paragraphs are, none the less, the material from which the walls and the wire topping them are made.

It is not the fault of the people behind the welfare and medical services that they are able to tackle prisoners' problems only if they are presented with them in a definite shape. The welfare department is like a messenger between the prisoner and his problem. Here I am with my problem; over there I see its solution. Can you help me? Yes, take a seat. Alcoholic? Try our Thursday-night Alcoholics Anonymous meeting. Kleptomaniac? See the psychiatrist. A love tangle, an impecunious relative, thwarted parole hopes, depression. . . . Solution? A telephone call (on the quiet, perhaps), extra social security allowance, uppers, downers. . . .

The system, in spite of its best intentions, determines that it shall be this way. Unfortunately, most problems affecting people in or out of prison are not capable of tidy definition; they are nebulous, too complex for simple sentences or else deeper than language, loose threads of the ragged self. What is named as 'the problem' might be no more than is caught by randomly clasping hands in a fog of suffering. The problem is what emerges from a pattern of being – a pattern which in these cases contrives consistently to produce disastrous results. To discover what or who created the pattern, it is unlikely to be enough to send someone to a discussion group, or to make an appointment with an overworked part-time psychiatrist. Chaplains, doctors and welfare officers are expert in their fields and mostly fired by high ideals, but their various attempts to call to the inner man are drowned by the regime, which first must restrict and contain the body before carrying out its other obligations.

The education department, while it cannot be expected to make uninterrupted efforts to confront prisoners with their deepest problems – its main task, after all, is to probe the mysteries of mathematics, history, art and other subjects – seemed a likely place where someone could at least begin asking the right questions about them; a stage which, necessarily, precedes the provision of the right answers.

It seems baffling at first that sections of the authorities have stood in the way of prisoners' education since it was introduced in the mid nineteenth century. In 1885, Sir Edmund DuCane, the Director of Prisons, was scornful of earlier attempts to teach literacy at Reading Prison:

> In this prison the inmates learned lessons all day . . . hard, heavy labour was absolutely forbidden in order that the whole attention might be devoted to literature – the establishment was a criminal university.

The Chaplain at the old prison in Lewes who left behind a notebook could have warned Sir Edmund of the dangers inherent in such study:

> Weston, F. a respected schoolmaster – Beginning of evils was – a Mr Walker made him read Voltaire, Hume, Paine – all sorts of Deistical books. Had then no antidote – Mind ever after unsettled.

That was in 1843. A prisoner reading Hume today is likely to be studying for a degree at the Open University, with the full backing of the Chaplain. But the inverted logic which was developed for the control of bodies is not to be overturned at a stroke – or even in a century and a half. A report by HM Chief Inspector of Prisons on Lewes Prison published in 1985 (based on an inspection in 1983) observed:

> The five classrooms available for basic education could have catered for between 40 and 50 young remand prisoners but agreements made with the local branch committee of the Prison Officers' Association had limited attendance to 25 each afternoon and revented evening classes for these inmates taking place. We regretted these restrictions on inmates who had few other activities in which to participate.

23 The Voice (IV): A Professional

The first time I went into his cell he sat me down comfortably, made a cup of coffee, placed a record of my choice on the turntable, wedged up the door and began rolling a joint.

'Thank you very much,' I said, 'but not for me.'

He was not put out. 'It's okay,' he replied, 'I'd be having one at this time anyway.'

It showed on his face, which was sallow and shadowed. He had a reputation for being uncooperative with staff, and probably held the distinction of being the prisoner most placed on report in the whole place.

But there was something else in his face: a wanting, a cry.

I liked him and he responded by visiting me regularly, bringing (unsolicited) bits of simple news, or else reporting back after yet another confrontation, or home leave. Having served most of an eight-year sentence, he was preparing to move to an open prison prior to release.

He had had enough of crime, he said, and brought me a letter from a businessman who stated his willingness to employ him; another was from a referee in the church.

I suspect that at first he thought I was one of 'them' – it is difficult for a long-term prisoner to conceive of strangers otherwise – and that he might gain by my influence. But finally he dropped that notion and we became friends.

'Round about May 1978 I used to frequent a public house in East London where various people who were involved in criminal activities associated and drank. While I was in the pub I was introduced to various people and over the course of two or three months had transactions with drugs, stolen property, chequebooks and cards, et cetera. One afternoon I was asked if I was interested in a burglary-type robbery where the victims would need to be, if they were inside the premises at the time, tied up or even guarded until whatever was in the house was taken. The address was put up as that of a prominent person who was chairman of a bank.

The following day with an accomplice, who had no previous convictions, I went to the address to look at the surrounding area and to keep an eye on the premises for a few hours to get a rough idea of the movements. It was a suburban-type area – basically, detached grounds with privet-hedge surrounds; the next-door house could have been no more than thirty yards away.

We both then, after spending the morning watching the premises, decided we'd need a van for the work we were about to carry out. I went and obtained a false driving licence and he went and hired a vehicle. Driving licences you can apply for in other people's names, dead people's names. You can steal them; you might find a driving licence when you're burgling a house; or someone else might burgle a house and find a driving licence and offer it to you. But whatever the means, obviously you don't use your own for hiring a vehicle.

We hired a vehicle with Kenning Van Hire, basically because these vehicles were hired out on contract to British Rail Parcels Services.

Our intention was that a limited amount of violence, if any, might have to be used, but it would not be necessary if no unfortunate errors took place: i.e., heroes. Because there's plenty of dead heroes. And also that I'm not a violent person; and when violence is totally unnecessary it only makes the crime, if one is caught, more serious, and obviously one must look at the consequences and possible penalties for your actions before committing an offence. Is it worth it? in other words.

We went to a British Rail Services depot about fifteen miles away from the actual area, made enquiries at their parcels desk. While the other guy was keeping the clerk busy, I managed to steal a clipboard belonging to BR, and on the clipboard were various consignment documents with people's addresses. Also I managed to steal a BR coat and cap. We didn't have a hired vehicle at that time. The vehicle we had was what in the trade they call a "ringer" – it was a stolen vehicle that had another number plate put on it, which was a legal number plate from a car which was the same year and model as the one we were driving, which was obviously stolen. Also we had stolen the tax disc from the car that we used the number from. Sometimes the owner notices; sometimes he just puts another tax disc in its place; sometimes you just put another tax disc in place and the owner never knows that he's got a bent tax disc.

This was safe in London to ferry around and very easily disposable of. If you burn the car out it can't be recognized – or only from engine numbers, fingerprints, that sort of thing.

The following day the vehicle was hired – on a Friday – it was hired out for the weekend, due back Monday, half-past two in the afternoon.

We used that vehicle over the weekend to take us to a location which would be suitable to go to after the robbery had been carried out, because if you drive for a long distance you might be stopped by the police, and the quicker you can empty the contents of the van, getting rid of the property that you've got, and maybe stocking-masks and gloves or whatever, then you cannot be charged with any offence. But while you're carrying the implements of crime with you, you can be stopped for a regular routine check and they've got the right to search the vehicle.

We managed to find a barn, which was out of the way, three or four miles from the location of the robbery which was to take place on the Monday morning.

Mr Roberts was sixty-eight and his wife was sixty-six. They weren't working people; they were upper-middle-class, or upper-class. They drove a Rolls-Royce and had a second car which was a Mercedes. As far as we knew they had no servants, because, as I say, over the weekend we watched the house.

There are many ways to watch a house: sometimes you can have a breakdown, where you actually call out a breakdown service and let them work on your vehicle – sabotage your own vehicle – so that you can watch the house. Sometimes you get people coming out, offering you cups of tea, maybe even asking you into their house to sit down and wait. Anyway, you get a rough idea of the area, so that you're not going in blind.

On the Monday we arrived at ten o'clock with the van. We were carrying no weapons at all. We were wearing no disguises other than the fact that I hadn't shaved for three or four days and my mate had a beard anyway. The police had no photographs of me at that time, as it wasn't statutory law for the police, if you were charged, to have a photograph record of you, other than the prison record of photographs, and I'd been out of prison, by then, for nearly a year.

I knocked on the front door, holding the clipboard. I was a little nervous, but determined. Everybody is frightened of the unknown, but I wasn't so nervous as to do something silly or go into a panic. I was level-headed, but obviously one does get butterflies.

My mate stayed in the van. We had managed to obtain some cardboard boxes over the weekend from a market. I went to the front door. Mr Roberts answered. I had a British Rail jacket on; my mate had the cap because he was going slightly bald, so as a disguise it was better

for him to have the cap on. Mr Roberts answered the door and I
explained to him that I was from the BR depot. He saw the board I was
carrying. We had altered the consignment notes to correspond with his
name and address. It didn't specify what the goods were but I'd got a
typewriter and typed in that they must be stored in a warm place, out of
damp air, preferably in dry warmth, inside.

Mr Roberts invited me into the house. I said just one moment, the
goods are in the van: I'll get the van backed up.

So my mate backed the van up to the front door, which was off a
small pathway about fifteen feet wide. The back van doors were open
and he started bringing in the empty cardboard boxes. I gave directions
where to put them.

While I was giving directions, obviously Mr Roberts's attention was
focused on my mate, because he had the goods and Mr Roberts was
curious to know what goods had been sent him. His wife then came out.
At this time, once all the boxes had been brought in, the front door was
closed and I asked Mr Roberts if he had a pen. While he went to get one,
my mate grabbed Mrs Roberts and held her in a bear-hug, told her she
was being robbed but that no one was going to be hurt.

I got a chair from the hall, sat her down and tied her hands to the
armrests. At this time her husband came back. He wasn't disabled,
exactly, but he wasn't an able enough person to be capable of putting
up a struggle if it came to it. Fortunately, it didn't. He accepted that he
was being robbed. His wife was a little bit annoyed that he should have
let us in. She kept saying: "Why did you let them in, why did you let
them in?"

Anyway, we sat Mr Roberts down, secured him to another chair and
told them both if they made any noise then we'd be forced to gag them.
Once they were secured, the telephone downstairs was put out of their
reach, for a start. Because if the phone rang and they kicked it off the
hook and screamed "Help!" then the alarm goes off.

We checked the house quickly to make sure there was nobody else in;
we also checked the back garden and the front, to make sure no one was
coming to the front door. My mate then went out, closed the van door
and came back inside.

I went immediately upstairs, found the safe, came back down, asked
him where the safe keys were. He told me where the safe keys were. I
went back upstairs, opened the safe. My mate came up, obviously –
didn't trust me, the bastard – we got the contents of the safe, which

were some jewellery and some cash: £14,000 in cash and various pieces of jewellery. Some turned out to be crystal, but they were antique crystal – given to the owners by Mountbatten.

We continued to search the house, taking any articles that were of value, such as silverware, paintings, carriage clocks, other articles of jewellery that women leave lying about on the dressing tables, in the kitchen, in jugs and so on. The owner also had an office there, which was to do with the bank, so we took various stamps and pay-in books, bankbooks, driving documents, credit cards – we took anything of value. These were all brought downstairs, put into the cardboard boxes that we brought. They were sitting watching us all the time.

We were in the house about fifteen or twenty minutes. The total value of the property was, with the paintings, just over £100,000: that is, retail or replacement value. On the open market . . . I mean, some criminals are cheated out of their loot quite easily because they've got no idea of the value of things and how to sell them. They've got no buyer and no idea where to get a buyer. They're desperate to get cash. Before I went on the robbery I was not desperate for cash. Also before I went on the robbery there were certain items in the house which were already sold – because inside information was given to us and certain articles were wanted. So we had sold the stuff before we nicked it, and the cash in the safe was a bonus. We knew about the crystal, we knew about the paintings and some candelabras, candlesticks, Georgian coffee services and so on.

When we left we went direct to a telephone box and made a call to the local police saying that there were people acting suspicious and could they come, there's been a disturbance. We gave the address. But, unbeknown to us, Mrs Roberts had managed to free her bonds and raise the alarm.

When the van was returned to the hire place – two days after the robbery – the police had a stake-out and they were waiting. The reason the van wasn't returned earlier was that the firearm which we found in the safe managed to go off, causing damage to the van. It was a Boer War revolver, 1898, no safety catch. The van was supposedly hired on a licence I'd obtained, but unbeknown to me my mate had lost the licence and, in his stupidity, used his own – because he was frightened to tell me that he'd lost the other one. He wasn't a professional thief, though with plenty of guts and plenty of intelligence. The upshot was, anyway, that he hired the van in his own name.

I went to the hire centre in another vehicle, behind my mate. Some of the property had been disposed of immediately, while other bits – Georgian tea services, a couple of paintings – were on the open market. I hadn't been prepared to accept the offer that the first person I'd gone to with it had made, so I was in the car with this stuff in the back, following my mate into the hire place.

When he came out, after having returned the van, he went to get into my car. The police came up and dragged us out – there was armed police everywhere. I had the firearm, I had the live ammunition in my top pocket. The firearm was in the car in a jacket pocket, unloaded.

My mate and I had done some business the previous evening with a man who was supposed to meet us after the van had been dropped off at the hire place, a few yards away in his own car, to do some transactions – paintings, silverware and other things. What I didn't know was that this man had been arrested but released back on to the street by the police, who were investigating robberies on banks and security guards delivering cash in transit to post offices. This man's girlfriend had apparently gone to the police and given them information of his involvement and he cooperated with the police fully. But while they thought he might commit another robbery with the people he'd committed the first ones with, the police were prepared to let him back on the street. So that when another robbery was about to be committed he would then give the police the information they needed and the robbers would be arrested on their way out of the bank.

However, this man gave the police information which led to our being charged. We were charged with various offences, but five of the six robberies we were charged with I didn't commit. My codefendant got half of everything I got: he was asked to go Queen's evidence against me but he refused. He received a year for possession of the firearm; I got two years. He got three years for the robbery; I got six.

I didn't feel sorry for the victims, other than the fact that they were elderly people. They were financially stable. Although they were classed as pensioners, they weren't drawing state pensions. The police tried to make out at the trial that we were preying on old people, but if a person's got half a million pounds in their bank account then they know that they are liable to burglary. Anybody that has a safe in their house must have something valuable.

This was a robbery-type burglary. Even though the minimum amount of force is used, the fact that you've tied people up is a threat of violence. It's classed as robbery, not burglary. In the court's eyes one is more serious than the other. No one was actually physically hurt. There may have been some mental hurt, but that could quite easily be compensated for – i.e., they'll get over it.

But if, say, Mrs Roberts was raped and her husband buggered, then they'll never get up. And there are people who commit these types of robberies that do go to these extremes. Why? They must be sick in the mind. But this robbery was planned, so that we knew the rough value of the property before we went in, we knew what we were going to get. It was a professional job – though only to an extent. It was an amateur job, because we got caught.'

24 The Spin

It was Gilbert's attempt to file his way through hell with a six-inch hacksaw blade that precipitated the great spin.

It took place on a Monday, a day I always spent in London, which all of the prisoners who gave me reports of it were convinced was deliberate, although I never tried to find out if this had substance.

What Gilbert didn't know, by the way, since no one had bothered to tell him, was that the bars on the window are saw-proof.

The spin, which was a talking point for weeks afterwards, involved the entire prison. Ostensibly it was a crackdown on lax security, a search for surplus property: unlisted or improperly listed items, which were, under orders, to be removed from the cells. If small enough they would be held in the property room at Reception; if not, then they would be confiscated, broken up and thrown away.

Not only was the raid on unofficial goods, but on the places to conceal them – to conceal anything. It is the intention of the prison authorities that the prisoner should have no refuge. As much as anything else, the spin was a renewed assault upon privacy.

In the son-of-the-chief's journal there was an account of the day's action:

Drama on the wing as cells are emptied of superfluous furniture. Three lads in revolt threw everything out of their cells and have been carted away. Many extra screws in evidence and much vitriolic language directed against them. Why oh why did I have to see the Chaplain smiling broadly at all the contraband furniture being loaded on to wagons?

Simon threw the TV over the landing and got put in the block. Tam threw *all* his furniture out and now has only a mattress on the floor. Dixie's cupboards – his proudest possession – were ripped off the walls and thrown out.

On a cell search a bloke's goldfish were discovered. He being told he couldn't have them threw the bowl and fish over the landing from the fours in a temper.

The rule book has been strictly applied, 'due to a serious breach of security': six books, one delft mug no more than 4″ high, no pictures on the back wall, one chair, one table, one locker, and so on. All surplus stuff had to be got rid of by a certain time or else it would be carted off and broken up – as it was: the rubbish filled three skips.

Apart from the obvious distress caused to inmates whose little homes have been devastated, I think the atmosphere is in a way healthy, rupturing as it does, if only for a short time, the incestuous cosy relationships that existed between Jailer and Jailed.

The new rigidity lasted well over a week; perhaps fully two. No one dared to take a step out of line, to handle anything which might be interpreted as contraband, or to say a word that could be construed as insubordinate. The hooch lay flat in its (unassailable) hiding places and the landings were curiously free of pungent aromas.

Then something happened. No one could say what started it off. Perhaps, to pay a debt – and debts have to be paid, no matter what the new regime looks like – the debtor offered to bring his chair over to another's cell that evening, and the creditor, mindful of the uses of an extra chair before giving thought to the present mood, agreed. Or it could have been a joke with a cutting edge between two people as a cell door was locked. Or maybe an exchange of radios, or batteries, or just of books.

The officers, if they were aware of it, treated it as a familiar, even welcome, sight – noisy children playing outside the kitchen window. Tired and weary after the great spin of a week or so before, they weren't ready to go searching cells for a seventh paperback or measuring delft mugs. So when whatever happened happened, nothing happened to contradict it.

Later, the sound of someone singing was heard from the showers and a joke was made about drunk and disorderly; a cloud floated out of Roger's cell; Muirfield's stereo system reasserted its claim to being the best – the loudest, that is – on the fours; Dixie began again the search for a decent set of cupboards, and Solomon decided, after much soul-searching, to remain on first-name terms with the screws in the kitchen. With each of these deals, another step was taken in repairing the shattered relationship between Jailer and Jailed. So it goes on.

25 Gate Fever

It's all done. Young Henry has been given his release date: 16 February.

From now until then, in three weeks' time, each minute will last an hour, every hour a day, and the days will drag out like weeks. Night will seem to him an opportunity to escape several hours of this time unconsciously, but he will find sleeping difficult.

Instead of sleeping, he will worry obsessively about things that could go wrong and obstruct his release: an officers' strike, a bureaucratic muddle, someone grassing him up over a minor and distant misdemeanour leading to loss of remission. . . .

It's called 'gate fever' and there isn't a prisoner approaching release who has not felt its grip. Now Young Henry will walk the landings with a heavy step, conscious of what the wrong move or word could bring down on him. Never have his actions been more responsible, his reasoning so pure. In his stronger moments he will resist the invitations into certain cells – the same invitations that have made these four years bearable – where sex or drugs, or both, are on offer.

The others will laugh at him, some kindly; others will talk cynically behind his back, begrudging any mention of his departure. His man will be bitter at this turning away, heartbroken over Young Henry's 'readjustment', seeing it as a betrayal in favour of the authorities. From now on, all efforts to talk to Young Henry will inevitably be converted to a single topic: his release.

The years had not visibly harmed Henry. He was a Scot, with red hair and gentle eyes and clear, almost translucent skin. He was twenty-seven and this was his second sentence. He had graduated from petty theft to burglary to armed robbery, in the time-honoured way. Now, as far as he was concerned, his life in prison was over. Already he spoke of it as part of history, referring to his current sentence in the past tense.

'I learned a lot from doing that sentence,' he said. 'In some ways it was good for me. The first sentence I did was a piece of cake: eighteen months for nine burglaries; served eleven of it without hardly blinking, and then out I went again, straight back to the same old places and the same old ways.'

The same old ways produced the same old result. Young Henry stormed into a house he thought was a goldmine, wielding a sawn-off shotgun, wearing a stocking-mask, the lot. The gun wasn't loaded – 'I wouldn't do anything like that,' he said – but it was still a gun. The police interviewed him the next day, and in spite of the stocking-mask he was recognized. Anyway, they found the stolen property under his bed.

To make the pill more bitter, the place hadn't been a goldmine at all. Henry got seven years for less than a thousand quids' worth.

'As I say, it's been good for me. What I feel is that you're better off with nothing outside than being in one of these places with nothing.'

I asked Young Henry if he intended to return to Scotland when he was released. He shook his head. His parents were up there, and his brother. They all wanted him back but he wouldn't go. He wouldn't think of returning to Scotland unless he was 'well off'.

What did he mean by that?

'I'd like to have a house by Loch Lomond, with a boat and water skis and so on. Join one of these clubs, that sort of thing. Otherwise . . .' – he made a rhetorical gesture with his arms akimbo – 'there's nothing else up there.'

That could wait. Young Henry had more immediate plans. Inside, he had met an older man, Ricky, who was serving a brief sentence because of some petty tax fiddling. Ricky was a plumber who had always had his own business, employing perhaps two or three men at most, and Henry – who had begun a plumber's apprenticeship in Glasgow but quit without completing it – was going to go into business with him.

'People in here,' he said with an air of exasperation, 'they talk about nothing but crime – jobs they've done, jobs they're going to do, even the jobs the people they know are doing right now.' He shook his head. 'I don't believe half of it anyway, but it bores the pants off you just the same. To hell with all that. I don't even go near these people any more.'

Most nights he just sat up in his own cell having a quiet smoke with Ricky, talking about the business – the future.

Whether it was these virtues, or something else, which impressed the Parole Board, Henry was granted parole. And, as a prelude to his release, he was given four days' home leave, which he spent with a relative who lived in Brighton.

When he returned to the prison after it was over, he called in to see me to relate the strange experience of the past four days. He looked different already: he had had a decent haircut, which ought to have made him smart, though in fact it only exaggerated his overall air of shock by giving him the appearance of someone who had been rudely cropped.

For the first time in four years and a month, he had stepped on a bus, walked through a shop door in a crowd, felt coins in his pockets, eaten a hot meal, ordered a drink in a pub, had a crease in his trousers and a shine on his shoes. But instead of making him happy, the experience left him raw and vulnerable.

'I was lost,' he said frankly. 'The prices! Christ, on Friday night I took my aunt and a couple of mates to the pub for a drink. I'll get the first one, boys, says I. Gives the guy a quid. Thanks, he says, I'll need another three of these. Four quid! For a round of drinks! I couldn't believe it.'

He couldn't work the telephones, one-man buses foxed him, the traffic frightened him, politeness from strangers embarrassed him, and there were policemen everywhere.

'Two hundred quid I spent when I was out,' he said with an air of bewilderment as if talking about something that had happened to someone else. 'Two hundred bloody quid – in four days!' He shook his head as if giving the spendthrift a good telling-off. 'I mean, that's ridiculous.'

A day or two later, he told me the same story again.

'Three hundred quid I spent. In four days. Three hundred!'

For the last fortnight of his time, Young Henry was given a job outside the walls, where he could work unsupervised. He had to clean up the driveway and gardens in front of the main gate. It was a good job to have. The sixteenth of February was not far away and getting closer, as he bathed himself in the almost-free air of the prison drive, saluting visitors and legal representatives on their way to see the less fortunate, eyeing the girlfriends, with even a chance of meeting an old aquaintance from the out as he made his way to visit someone else. But that, of course, could be dangerous.

I met him in front of the gate on the afternoon of the day before he was due to go, a Friday. The air was mild and you could feel spring on its way. A good time to be going. Henry took a welcome break from his task and leaned on the handle of his broom. He repeated the story about his big spending once more – it had stuck at three hundred – shaking his head in disbelief in the same way, to illustrate his helplessness in the face of natural extravagance.

Then he grew philosophical again.

'You don't need all these things, you know: girls and big cars and flashy clothes and jewellery, money to buy all your friends drinks. That isn't happiness. It's no good to you if you haven't got your freedom. All that glitters is not gold.'

Henry turned out the old cliché as if it were an original thought. Then he rehearsed his favourite slogan again:

'Better on the out with nothing than being in one of these places with the same amount. Right? I tell that to these guys in there, but all they can talk about is crime, crime. . . . Crime means time, if you ask me. I'll tell you this: this sentence has taught me something: crime *doesn't* pay. Right?'

Right. We shook hands. I wished him luck. Then I left, while he continued to sweep the driveway, as if cleaning it in preparation for his own departure.

In the morning Henry was unlocked and escorted to Reception. There he sloughed off the prison grey in the same doggie-box where he had changed into it, seeing the same officers before him and the same orderlies passing back and forth; but it was happening now in reverse – the same images speeded up and run backwards. In the remnants lying on the floor at his feet he saw not a former self but a number. N84621 was dead.

He changed into his own clothes; he felt the awkward but familiar position of the pockets and tested them with his hands; these green trousers, new then, which he had worn to go to court; that patterned shirt – like the shoes less fashionable now than when last worn; comforting, welcoming, both a reminder of the nearly lost and harbinger of the yet-to-be-found.

He picked up his belongings, which had been packed the previous day and checked at Reception for contraband. Then he signed the Firearms Act. Two days earlier, before the Governor, he had signed his release papers, like any other prisoner released on licence. He was given the standard £27.50 subsistence and a travel warrant to get him to Brighton.

The Senior Officer remembered to say goodbye as he walked out of Reception, under escort for the last time, to the main gate. No one was there to welcome him to freedom, but Young Henry didn't mind that. He walked down the drive he had been sweeping clean for the previous fortnight. To hell with that. Someone else could do it now. He reached the traffic lights – the first beacon of freedom – and crossed the road without waiting for the green man. He looked about him: it was early and there was no one around; a shopkeeper was mopping the pavement in front of his shop; it was Saturday, there was open air and open space and a train waiting at the platform to take him to Brighton.

It was Ricky, the business partner, who told me. I came across him standing outside the wing office. He was waiting to put in another of his hopeless requests to be allowed a telephone call. We had exchanged pleasantries on a number of occasions, but usually he seemed too shy, or broken, to want to talk at length. His sentence, though it was a short one, had dealt him a serious hurt. He had served it from the inside.

'He's back,' he said.

'Who?'

'Young Henryson.'

'No!'

'He's in F Wing, on remand. Eleven days he lasted. Stupid young fool.' Ricky had a half-smile on his lips, which I knew was merely an effect of his stoicism. He was genuinely angered and sorry. 'Eleven bloody days.'

The charge was burglary. For this he had to endure not only the contempt of the prison staff and probation officers who had wished him well and patted his shoulders over the past weeks, brightening at his talk of sharing a business with Ricky, but also the scorn of his erstwhile wingmates. As a remand prisoner, he would be kept in F Wing until sentencing – he was pleading guilty, according to Ricky – and would see the others only at church, or at odd moments when their paths crossed in the corridors on the way to education or kit change. In addition to whatever sentence was doled out to him, he would now have to serve the remainder of his previous sentence, since he had broken parole.

Poor Henry. His resolutions based on the nothing-outside-is-better-than-nothing-inside principle had no force when faced with the glamour he coveted. He had accepted all the messages of the consumer society at face value and should have been regarded as one of its most faithful accomplices, having taken its ethics entirely to heart. He had acted quite as the most convinced of its elders would have wished him to act: as a set of reflexive desires and appetites, with a belief, too deep to winkle out by reason alone, that all that glitters *is* gold.

Instead, however, because of a simple failure of method, he was reviled, captured and about to be punished. When all he wanted was a boat and a loch to sail it on.

But now he had gained renewed insight into that condition of being merely an acquisitive force. The price, however, was to see himself from the point of view of those who had incarcerated him and were preparing, even now, to reduce him to a body.

'This', he is supposed to have said, in the last report of him to reach me, 'is the best thing that ever happened to me.'

26 · The Body (III)

'I'll have the bodies ready for you.' The reification plagued my vocabulary, as images of cells and keys and uniformity flashed across my eyes and through my dreams at night. And I began to see the obsession which many cons had with physical fitness as a battle for linguistic as well as physical supremacy: '*I'll* have the body ready for *you*.'

One afternoon while I was sitting in the Assistant Governor's office, the Chaplain provided a macabre touch of humour, bringing home once again just how weirdly suitable this lexicon was.

He knocked first, then popped his head round the door to tell the Assistant Governor that he would be 'picking up the body at two o'clock tomorrow'.

I was dismayed, at first, to hear this; it's one thing for prison officers to refer to their charges as 'bodies', I thought, but quite another for the Chaplain to do so. It was not until later in the day that I discovered he had been talking about the weekend's suicide.

Singer — I never discovered his Christian name — had been transferred recently from another prison, where it had been decided that he was in need of psychiatric treatment. He was 'difficult', verging towards 'uncontrollable'.

At Lewes, they kept him in the hospital wing as a suicide risk, under a fifteen-minute watch. Every quarter of an hour an officer would march up to his cell door, slip the shield from the judas eye, and spy on Singer — in order to see if, in the system's own colloquialism, 'everything was all right with him'.

Singer must have felt that the sound of footsteps leading to his door, the sudden peep of light as the cover was removed, the appearance behind it of the disembodied eye, meant he was anything but 'all right'.

He was serious about what he was going to do and timed it to perfection.

After the last inspection passed and the cover slid into place again, Singer looped the slings of his vest round his neck and knotted the hem around the bars.

'. . . The poor wretch now shook violently, and opened and closed his hands in a convulsive manner. He could scarcely stand, and moved to and fro, exclaiming in a low and fervent tone . . . "Lord Jesus, receive my spirit!"'

Unlike John Murdock in 1856, Singer had no audience, nor a faithful reporter to provide him with local immortality by printing an account of his last hours in the newspaper. He died in silence; his obituary, an entry in a record book and some intimations of regret among senior prison staff.

Some weeks later I was in the property room at Reception, where prisoners' belongings are stored for the duration of their stay. The officer I was talking to pointed out a small pile which stood apart from the rest on the floor, consisting of three cardboard boxes.

'These belonged to a young man who killed himself,' the officer said. 'This stuff can't be touched or taken away from here until there's been a coroner's report.'

On front of the brown box on the top of the pile was written, in large letters with a felt-tip pen: SINGER; and, below it, a number. There wasn't much in the boxes: a pair of small speakers belonging to a record player, some records, a pair of spectacles, a miniature New Testament, bits of clothing. . . .

'Here,' the officer lifted a swatch of colour photographs out of the shambles, 'you might be interested in looking at these.'

I took them. The first was of an attractive black woman and two children. It was taken in a clean and tidy kitchen, and all were laughing. But what he meant me to look at was underneath: two photographs of the same woman dressed in bright red camiknickers and net stockings. She was lounging on a sofa in one photograph, and on the floor in the other. In the first, legs astride, she held the fingers of one hand against her pudendum, without exposing it, and had a coy, take-me smile on her lips and in her eyes. In the other photograph she was doing something similar with the right hand while raising a banana to her lips with the left.

I kept looking at them, even though I was conscious of the officer looking at me. The whole background to the pictures was suddenly present in my apprehension of their passage from having been a private delight to becoming a public spectacle. I saw why she had had them taken, what she was thinking about when the shutter closed, why she wanted him to have them, and how she had wondered about their fate when hearing the news of his death.

I continued to look at this very pretty woman, turning from the first to the second and back again. I found them terribly, vividly erotic; she was flesh and heart and voice, and her laughter resisted and repulsed all others' fantasies of how a body ought to be. She was laughing in the kitchen, and for an instant — a gap in my awareness of the officer, the room, the cell, the keys, the kit, the uniform, the block, the reports, the wall, the gate — I heard her loud, joyful laugh.

'Macabre, moony and plain strip-joint sleazy'
SUNDAY TIMES

SNOW WHITE AND ROSE RED
by ED McBAIN

Sarah Whittaker, said her attorney, was nuttier than a fruitcake. When Matthew Hope visited her in the institution he was half-expecting some shaven-headed basket case in a uniform that looked like mattress ticking.

Instead Sarah Whittaker was wearing a wheat-coloured linen suit and a saffron silk blouse open at the throat. She had a generous mouth and eyes as green as the Amazon jungle and Matthew Hope fell in love with her on the spot.

'So why are you here?' he asked. 'Ah,' she said, and started to tell him a story. And it certainly wasn't the kind of tale a mother would read to her children at bedtime . . .

'A swift and adroitly plotted mystery . . . events leave the reader devastated'.
PUBLISHERS WEEKLY

'Laces its horrors with some good running gags and some gamey writing . . . everything one looks for in vintage McBain'.
THE FICTION MAGAZINE

0 7221 5726 6   CRIME   £2.95

A CLASSIC CRIME THRILLER . . .

THE SENTRIES

ED McBAIN

Jason Trench had had it up to here with the way those Commies were giving his country the runaround. If the politicos weren't going to get up off their fat butts and do something then he sure as hell would. He wanted action *now*.

Jason wasn't just some patriotic fruitcake who'd seen one too many John Wayne movies. Jason had a plan. He had forty-two loyal men behind him and they were even crazier than he was. He didn't need speeches or slogans.

He had guns. And he used them . . .

0 7221 5762 2   CRIME   £2.95

Also by Ed McBain in Sphere Books:
JACK AND THE BEANSTALK
SNOW WHITE AND ROSE RED

Close Her Eyes

DOROTHY SIMPSON

Winner of the Silver Dagger Award

News that an innocent young girl like Charity Pritchard is
missing will pierce the armour of policemen far more
hard-bitten than Inspector Thanet. And his concern deepens
when the first thought of her family – strict religious
fundamentalists – is to leave the matter in God's hands.

Of course no detective worth his salt will put much faith
in outward appearances. And he is hardly likely to pay much
heed to first impressions. But it will be a good while after
Inspector Thanet finds Charity's poor broken body before
he realises just how wrong his preconceptions can be . . .

0 7221 7874 3   CRIME   £2.50

Also by Dorothy Simpson in Sphere Books:
PUPPET FOR A CORPSE

A selection of bestsellers from Sphere:

FICTION

THE SECRETS OF HARRY BRIGHT	Joseph Wambaugh	£2.95 ☐
CYCLOPS	Clive Cussler	£3.50 ☐
THE SEVENTH SECRET	Irving Wallace	£2.95 ☐
CARIBBEE	Thomas Hoover	£3.50 ☐
THE GLORY GAME	Janet Dailey	£3.50 ☐

FILM & TV TIE-IN

INTIMATE CONTACT	Jacqueline Osborne	£2.50 ☐
BEST OF BRITISH	Maurice Sellar	£8.95 ☐
SEX WITH PAULA YATES	Paula Yates	£2.95 ☐
RAW DEAL	Walter Wager	£2.50 ☐

NON-FICTION

URI GELLER'S FORTUNE SECRETS	Uri Geller	£2.50 ☐
A TASTE OF LIFE	Julie Stafford	£3.50 ☐
HOLLYWOOD A' GO-GO	Andrew Yule	£3.50 ☐
THE OXFORD CHILDREN'S THESAURUS		£3.95 ☐
THE MAUL AND THE PEAR TREE	T. A. Critchley & P. D. James	£3.50 ☐

All Sphere Books are available at your local bookshop or newsagent, or can be ordered direct from the publisher. Just tick the titles you want and fill in the form below.

_____

Name_____

Address_____

_____

Write to Sphere Books, Cash Sales Department, P.O. Box 11, Falmouth, Cornwall TR10 9EN.
Please enclose a cheque or postal order to the value of the cover price plus:
UK: 60p for the first book, 25p for the second book and 15p for each additional book ordered to a maximum charge of £1.90.
OVERSEAS & EIRE: £1.25 for the first book, 75p for the second book and 28p for each subsequent title ordered.
BFPO: 60p for the first book, 25p for the second book plus 15p per copy for the next 7 books, thereafter 9p per book.
Sphere Books reserve the right to show new retail prices on covers which may differ from those previously advertised in the text elsewhere, and to increase postal rates in accordance with the P.O.